4.50

/GN397.5.A64>C1/

Date Due

ist

DISCARD

Do Applied Anthropologists Apply Anthropology?

Do
Applied
Anthropologists
Apply Anthropology?

MICHAEL V. ANGROSINO, EDITOR

Southern Anthropological Society
Proceedings, No. 10

SOUTHERN ANTHROPOLOGICAL SOCIETY
Distributed by the University of Georgia Press
Athens 30602

Southern Anthropological Society

Founded 1966

Copyright © 1976 by the Southern Anthropological Society
All rights reserved

Library of Congress Catalog Card Number: 75-32126
International Standard Book Number: 0-8203-0393-3

Set in 10 on 12 pt. Janson type
Printed in the United States of America

Contents

Preface

THE present symposium asks, "Do Applied Anthropologists Apply Anthropology?" and with surprising consensus the symposium participants answer, "Yes, but. . . ." In their separate affirmations and modifications lie the lessons of the papers that follow. The papers were first read at the key symposium of the tenth annual meeting of the Southern Anthropological Society, held at Clearwater Beach, Florida, April 3-5, 1975, hosted by the Department of Anthropology of the University of South Florida. Special thanks go to Michael V. Angrosino, the meeting's program coordinator, and J. Raymond Williams, in charge of local arrangements.

With this issue I end my term as SAS Proceedings editor, transferring the series into the good hands of Gwen Neville.

Irma Honigmann
SAS Editor

The Evolution of
the New Applied Anthropology

Michael V. Angrosino

This symposium developed out of the efforts of members of the Department of Anthropology at the University of South Florida to operationalize its new M.A. program in applied anthropology. My colleagues and I were responding to the need we perceived to train professional anthropologists for nonacademic employment, in part because of the dwindling job market in academic anthropology (Kushner and Angrosino 1974).

As the program developed, we became aware that although applied anthropology has a long tradition and accommodates many types of applications, certain kinds of applied work seem to be typical of the applied anthropology being done currently. This "new" applied anthropology relies on short-term, contract work in public service agencies, work often involving program evaluation, and work that can often be undertaken off campus. Because such work seemed so different from the traditional research we learned in graduate school—in conception, in method, in utilization—and because our continued identification as anthropologists was important to us, we began to wonder about the continuity between traditional anthropology (even traditional applied anthropology) and the new applied anthropology. Hence, the original idea for the symposium.

The evolution we perceived in applied anthropology toward different emphases (albeit not necessarily totally new concerns) generated some thought about the process of continuity and change within the discipline over several professional generations. Many of the pioneers of applied anthropology saw their discipline as more than a mere science—it was virtually a gospel that could be used to underwrite better human relations all over the globe. True, these early anthropologists often acted as agents of policies that turned out to be not notably humanitarian in their eventual execution, however noble they may have been in conception. Exclusively concerned with "their people," they failed to take a corresponding interest in the bureaucracies that employed them. The fatal flaw in the anthropological grand design for world brotherhood was the inability of anthropologists to extend the same courtesies shown their exotic subjects to the white European and American administrators. Few anthropologists felt it to be within their purview to study a bureaucratic system to find out how it worked, and why sometimes—despite the best of intentions—it worked against the interests of the people it served. Although they derided social scientists preoccupied with Western societies for ignoring "the other half of the world," anthropologists all too frequently saw the world through the other end of the telescope, from the point of view of primitive, isolated, tribal peoples. With occasional exceptions, anthropologists failed to understand their own most important message—that we are all of us involved in the world together, the white bureaucrat and the exotic "savage" alike. Because of their unwillingness to study the Euro-American part of this equation with the same devotion applied to the primitive, anthropologists could not act as mediators between the two cultures. Their service, then, was hollow, and the colonialists cannot be blamed for misunderstanding and misusing the anthropological message they were supposed to have been absorbing.

World War II helped crystallize the notion of service in many segments of the American population. Social scientists were mobilized to aid the war effort directed against a far more coherent threat to international brotherhood than the colonialists of Africa. During this period, anthropologists transferred their crusading, optimistic moralism of the earlier period to a series of pragmatic tasks directed toward a definite and realizable goal—winning the war. This "can-do" spirit survived the war itself, and throughout the rest of the 1940's and 1950's, applied anthropology came to be thought of as a sort of task-oriented service, the application of sensible, empirically grounded observations to specific problems. That these activities were almost exclusively in the service of what came to be known as the military-industrial complex was not considered a handicap in those days. Like the British anthropologists in colonial Africa, these war-era anthropologists overlooked the nature of the institutions they served, convinced that their own humanitarian goals were sufficiently worthy in and of themselves.

Despite the foundation of the Society for Applied Anthropology during this period, this branch of the discipline was considered a lesser kind of anthropology. Like an aristocratic family going into trade to keep up payments, applied anthropologists were felt to be simplifying the complex wisdom of their craft and getting their hands dirty in service. As the wartime optimism faded, and as it became clearer that improving the rapport within an assembly-line crew did nothing to ameliorate the problems of the industrial system at large, applied anthropology became the ugly stepsister within the discipline. It became an act of condescension in many cases, rather than an act of conviction for the anthropologist to descend from the ivory tower to solve problems.

The dissatisfaction with standard applied anthropology—its limited potential for meaningful service and its status as watered-down anthropology that contributed little to either theory or method—was answered, in part, by those action anthropology classics, the Fox and Vicos projects. The latter's focus on directed culture change represents a significant shift in strategy, a markedly different relationship between academic social science and the real world from that represented by traditional applied anthropology.

By the late 1960's, the anthropological profession had become acutely conscious of the ethical implications of fieldwork, particularly in applied projects. The radical movements of the decade questioned the classic concept of the liberal arts education and the notion that learning was a goal unto itself; rather, one had to be educated *for* something, and courses had to be relevant to the real world, not in the older sense of preparation for a job, but in the sense of being equipped to challenge society in meaningful ways.

Anthropology has long led a sheltered existence as the exotic social science that outsiders never really expected to be relevant to anything modern or useful. Although anthropologists themselves were aware of their discipline's involvement in the world, and despite the doubts and criticisms they expressed about the political and social ethics of research, anthropology had a relatively clean reputation and could be expected to step in where other social sciences had failed.

This, needless to say, was a very dangerous position for the discipline, since for the first time in its history it was moving into areas of endeavor not for scholarly or generalized humanitarian motives but out of political necessity. Moreover, it was now required to put up or shut up. In an earlier era, failure could be dismissed as regrettable, but failed anthropology in this newly politicized context constituted a political blunder with ramifications outside the confines of academic research.

The Radical Caucus within American anthropology, which emerged during this period, helped to focus attention on two distinct but related issues. In the first place, the radicals pointed out, although professional ethics traditionally meant such things as not exposing the identity of one's informants and reimbursing people for interview time, this ethic was essentially immoral. It was a negative ethic designed to protect one's subjects in a paternalistic fashion and to avoid controversy. But controversy—in the form of politicized confrontation—was the primary goal of the radical politics of the 1960's, and an ethical stand negating a scientist's obligation to be controversial, to raise issues that would indeed cause trouble for the established order, was no ethic at all.

A new emphasis was placed on the moral ambiguity inherent in the anthropologists' traditional avoidance of involvement in or understanding of the bureaucracies out of which they worked. Such avoidance had helped keep the profession relatively clean, to be sure, but it also made anthropologists impotent Candides, blissfully unaware of the ways in which the dominant institutions of their own culture manipulated their lives and the lives of "their" natives. As a result, anthropological research was not merely self-serving and irrelevant; it could be construed as downright criminal. By puritanically refusing to be contaminated by involvement in the bureaucratic superstructure, anthropologists shut themselves off from the knowledge that would be most profitable for "their" people. They could not teach peasants, for example, as much about dealing with bureaucrats as they could, even unwittingly, teach bureaucrats about dealing with peasants. In the radical view, applied anthropology, whatever its expressed purpose, became nothing but a means by which those in power could tighten their grip on the downtrodden.

The radical program aimed to make anthropology's traditional sympathies for the underdog into a meaningful political position: action anthropology became advocacy anthropology, the attempt to discern what the "little man" really wanted and to help him achieve his goals rather than to countenance his victimization by those in power.

One views with rueful amusement the naiveté of a position that only a few short years ago seemed so boldly inflammatory. Despite its aim of reaching out beyond the campus to solve the problems of the world, radical anthropology's solution turned on the old grade-school notion of the power of education to uplift, a sentiment that would have been laughed out the window were it stated in its pure form. What, after all, did the anthropologists' "advocacy" imply if not a process whereby dedicated scholars taught the techniques of confrontation and revolution to poor, eager peasants? It was the Régis Debray revolutionary syndrome: the intellectual as spiritual mentor to political upheaval. The practical problem of how, for example, anthropologists would do counter-counterinsurgency work on a military junta for the benefit of the waiting *campesinos* was never really solved.

The radical anthropologists were as naive in their belief that political and social revolution could grow out of an anthropology textbook as earlier action anthropolgists were in believing that they could ignore the bureaucracy. An anthropologist could, of course, be a genuine revolutionary, but a true revolutionary is rarely an academic professional; one might be a revolutionary with training in anthropology, but revolution is an act of politics, not of scholarship as commonly defined. A critical dilemma crystallized: is applied research possible at all? If one does academically sound research, one risks being politically reactionary, or worse; but if one makes a revolutionary difference in a given social situation, one is no longer doing research as traditionally understood. For the radicals of the 1960's, the choice was clear: down with traditional academicism!

In the exhaustion characteristic of the politics of the 1970's, anthropology stopped short of its logical ends. But pressed by the economic crises of the decade, the profession grasped one message: anthropologists must either be willing to take up nontraditional positions (positions other than teaching or basic research), or they will not work as anthropologists at all. Applied anthropology—once a fringe effort of academia, and later the putative spearhead of political and social action—is now back in vogue, albeit in a new guise. No longer is it considered vulgarly unintellectual to ask, "But what kind of job can I get with a degree in anthropology?" Applied anthropology is now a valid alternative as a career, not merely a sideline to "real" anthropology.

What, then, is the new applied anthropology, and who are the new anthropologists venturing into the nonacademic world? Ironically, virtually without exception, every faculty member in every anthropology department in the United States and Canada was trained in an academic setting within the classic traditions of Boas, Radcliffe-Brown, and the rest. The holistic, four-field approach and the emphasis on prolonged fieldwork are in the bones. And yet these very people are now expected to work off campus (not necessarily in research) or, more important, to train students who will be fully qualifiied to take up permanent positions as anthropologists in the world.

The first task of the new applied anthropology is to define a focus of activity (Redfield 1973). Anthropology has been forced to look seriously at its own society, a society, ironically, most anthropologists are least equipped, by training or instinct, to deal with.

Their discipline, most anthropologists would agree, has just as much to contribute to the study of contemporary America as do the other social sciences. The anthropological perspective, they point out, enables us to look at people in a total way. But the gap between a perspective and a job that could make use of that perspective seems very wide indeed. Many potential employers, if they think of anthropology at all, have images of Turhan Bey in the mummy's tomb, Jane Goodall's striking poses in the *National Geographic,* and Margaret Mead's discussing sex on the David Susskind show. Even those aware of the applied tradition link it to the administration of Indian reservations or to other exotica.

How, then, can we convince potential employers that anthropologists constitute an employable resource pool? Many in the discipline talk about the pressing need to develop off-campus, untraditional employment possibilities, yet few confront the inherent challenge to the basic assumptions we absorbed as anthropologists trained in the "old school."

Social service agencies offer no insurmountable resistance to anthropology, although most professionals (in the health care fields, for example) are suspicious of any academic discipline claiming to have something new to sell. This suspicion is related to a dilemma that most advocates of the new applied anthropology have not yet faced, although the members of the American Anthropological Association Manpower Committee expressed it, perhaps unintentionally, in their now-famous quip about the buffalo's disappearing. They were referring to the difficulty of selling anthropology as a job, and of the increased shortage of "subsistence" for trained anthropologists. It would seem, however, that the range of human social problems is so vast that there is no reason to despair of nothing left to do. In the pragmatic 1970's, we may all have finally discovered that no single discipline can do it alone (whatever "it" happens to be). We no longer need to emphasize the distinctiveness of the anthropological perspective in dealing with off-campus professionals. Social service agencies, which after all have definite tasks to perform, care little about the differences between sociology and anthropology, for instance. It is more important that they be made aware that social science, as well as "hard" science, belongs in their setting. With that point established, we will all have an equal shot at the buffalo.

The ramifications of this position are yet to be fully worked out. But undoubtedly most applied anthropologists would be willing to shift to this new, multidisciplinary frame of reference. Few social agencies can wait around for an ethnographer to do a year of participant observation before tackling the problem at hand; few have the money to support it. As a result, the new applied anthropology, in the agency setting, must perforce be "quick-and-dirty" survey work, the sort of thing anthropologists have traditionally sneered at sociologists and social psychologists for indulging in.

It is, furthermore, very difficult to fund applied research using the standard grant approach; one must now think in terms of the contract rather than the grant. Most traditional granting sources permit the researcher considerable flexibility in developing the eventual parameters of research. But when an agency, such as a county planning commission, contracts for a specified piece of work, it is indeed a contract, often signed by the university, with the researcher and his or her staff merely the agents of the university administration. Under the terms of the contract, the researcher and team must file a specified report on a specified topic to be handed in on a specified date.

Working in one's own local area, within a very restricted time schedule, primarily as an administrator of money dispersed to a research staff, and rarely getting out "among the people" are all new constraints posing difficult adjustments for the new anthropologist trained in the old anthropology. But probably more bitter is the realization that the work being done is not research at all in the sense that anthropologists have come to understand it. In the subfield of medical anthropology, for example, one of the long-standing areas of interest has been the ethnography of health care service. The anthropologist traces out who provides which services, who utilizes them, and how those services are ramified throughout a given community system. Traditionally, such a study meant living in the community and reporting its perceived needs to the health professionals (who either accepted or rejected suggestions according to their own needs). However, agencies need to make the most efficient use of their money and time, and this often means hiring a staff to interview only the health professionals about a community's health needs. How an agency translates that information in applying it to the target community is left as ambiguous as how the community's needs were translated to the professionals in the earlier phases of research.

Thus, in just a few short years, the exigencies of the current economic situation are leading anthropologists into new forms of application and toward a sharp reversal of their values. For the first time, applied anthropology qualifies as a valid career alternative for the professional anthropologist, not as a sideline to a career in academia. But this new career orientation runs counter to the socialization experienced by most professionals in graduate schools that instilled the values of traditional academic anthropology and that provided a reward system to reinforce those values.

What, then, happens to us as we begin to operate in the off-campus world of service agencies and the like—a world so different from academia in operation, in style, in assumptions, and with its own system of expectations and rewards? How do we inculcate those nonacademic values and attitudes in our students as we gear up for training programs rather than (or, at least, in addition to) traditional graduate education, when we ourselves are experiencing culture shock in the face of those new values and attitudes? From being scientists who understood the natives *au fond* and the bureaucrats not at all, we have become bureaucrats ourselves, talking wistfully about getting our newly found knowledge back to the people, sometime, somehow.

New applied anthropology is not carried like missionary gospel to the waiting world, but is offered to a world that defines and restricts the limits in which anthropology can function. The question arises, therefore: Can an academic discipline survive when its special body of theory and method is lost sight of in multifaceted endeavors? Is there a core of anthropology that we can carry on even in short-term contract work, unrecognizable perhaps from what we were taught in graduate school, but that enables us to make a special contribution to dealing with social problems?

No real stock-taking of applied anthropology has ever been done—we have been content with an accretion of projects and studies and data. But if we are, in fact, emerging as a distinctive professional category, the ambiguities of our identity should be dealt with. In drawing together for this symposium various professionals who have thought through that problem and in presenting their strategies for coping with it, we will have begun to come to grips with the questions of who we are and why we think we can sell our special skills.

REFERENCES

Kushner, Gilbert, and Michael V. Angrosino, 1974. Applied Anthropology at the University of South Florida. In *Training Programs For New Opportunities in Applied Anthropology*, E. Leacock, N. L. Gonzalez, and G. Kushner, eds. (Washington D.C.: American Anthropological Association), pp. 34-38.

Redfield, Alden, ed., 1973. *Anthropology Beyond the University*, Southern Anthropological Society Proceedings, No. 7 (Athens: University of Georgia Press).

The Art of Practicing Anthropology

JOHN BUSHNELL

LOOKING back to the recently ended period of expansion in anthropology, we might say with tongue in cheek that in some respects this phase resembled the operation of a cat-and-rat farm. Those were the days when graduate departments of anthropology produced Ph.D.'s who were then hired to staff new or expanding departments in order to produce more Ph.D.s to serve as professors to more graduate students. Eventually and inevitably supply had to overtake and outrun demand. At present, job opportunities in the academic world have dwindled to a trickle and there has been a near-panic reaction in some quarters calling, in effect, for a policy verging on zero growth. In addition to this unsettling state of affairs, the traditional image of the anthropologist as professor/researcher has been shaken by demands from the radical activist sector for relevancy, accountability, and advocacy, modes of functioning that are best realized off campus. In the light of these two divergent influences, one a bread-and-butter matter, the other essentially ideological, it would appear that growth in anthropology in the foreseeable future will occur primarily in areas customarily subsumed under applied anthropology. Given the liklihood, therefore, that many novitiates in our discipline will eventually be operating in applied fields, we are brought face to face with such problems as: how do we train this new genre of anthropologist and how will these developing careers fit into the established status hierarchy (or must they?) with its long-standing image of academia as the ultimate in professional purpose and life-style?

In an effort to shape the future we not infrequently have recourse to the past. One source of potentially useful data resides in those of us who have worked or are now working as anthropologists in positions outside the college and university circuit. In this connection I will draw upon certain aspects of my own years in anthropology, presenting in capsule form the experience of functioning as an anthropologist in two markedly different applied settings. I will then consider the relevance of graduate training vis-a-vis employment outside the boundaries of traditional anthropology and, finally, offer some thoughts regarding the direction in which I believe anthropology may be moving, and perhaps has to move, in terms of both self-concept and training if our discipline is to meet its potential. Here I refer not only to the expansion of job opportunities but also to the contribution anthropology can make to the solution of human problems.

The mid-1950's paralleled the mid-1970's as a time of relative overproduction of anthropologists, which made job-hunting especially trying for new Ph.D.s. After a one-year stint on an interim teaching appointment at Vassar College, I moved into the position of research associate for the Mary Conover Mellon Foundation program, a longitudinal, psychologically oriented research project focusing on the educational process at Vassar. I was confident that anthropology could make a significant contribution to the understanding of how and why the students responded to the college experience as they did. I began by assigning myself the title of staff anthropologist in a move to shore up my identity, since I found myself in a professional milieu in which I was essentially a stranger. Research activity was in full swing at the time I joined the project and I was immediately immersed in a team approach structured by psychologists in which it was expected that all hands would share in the large-scale interviewing program, in the administration of personality inventories, and in the analysis, interpretation, and write-up of interview and correlational data. Given these expectations there were obviously many critical gaps in my background and I had to augment informal on-the-job learning with a crash program designed to fill myself in on the idiom, modes of thinking, and research approaches of the psychologist, not to mention a first approximation to conceptualizing the capabilities of the computer.

When I reached a level of expertise that allowed me to breathe more easily, I proposed a study of campus culture that was specifically anthropological in concept and approach in which the interaction between two subcultures, faculty/administration and student, was conceived in terms of a culture contact situation. The plan was approved and added to the overall design, albeit somewhat as an appendage. I was free to carry out my proposal with the left hand, so to speak. At this point a key stratagem was denied me. I had hoped to live among the "natives," i.e., in one of the dorms in the role of house fellow, a position in which a faculty member served as counselor

and confidant to the students. Notwithstanding this setback, there
were sufficient opportunities to carry out a field study based on participant observation and interview in the tradition of the lone anthropologist, and Vassar campus culture subsequently assumed an appropriate place in the analysis of the Vassar student (Bushnell 1959,
1960, 1962, 1964).

With the phasing out of the Mellon Foundation program, I accepted a position as director of research for the New York State
Commission for Human Rights headquartered in New York City.
It is essential to note here that for this job I was not hired primarily
as an anthropologist, nor was I regarded as such except by a few
close associates in the agency. Rather, I was chief of the Research
Division and was expected to provide the research expertise that
could generate the data, analyses, conclusions, and recommendations
deemed essential to the functioning of the commission. The work
centered largely on statistical analyses—complaint records, census data,
employment patterns, and so forth. An occasional field survey utilizing
interview schedules would be conducted for the purpose of investigating, for example, the nature and scope of discriminatory practices
in the resort areas of the Catskills. In addition, the division maintained a twenty-four-hour service capable of providing commissioners,
the executive director, or other division heads with whatever information was needed to complete a speech, to frame a reply to charges
in the media, or to provide a statistical justification in support of an
upcoming program or action to be announced by the agency.

There were occasions when an anthropologically or sociologically
oriented study would have been feasible, but proposals of this order
were all too often disapproved on grounds that the findings would
not be relevant to the immediate needs of the commission or that
problems would be spotlighted at a time when the agency was not
prepared to cope with them. Potential research projects seem to
have been most often pragmatically evaluated in terms of ultimate
public relations value, e.g., would the findings demonstrate that the
commission was doing a bigger, if not always a better, job this year
than last? In short, the modus operandi of the Commission for
Human Rights either precluded or effectively discouraged any large-
scale incorporation of anthropological approaches into its research
activities. Predictably, I became progressively more frustrated and
alienated, notwithstanding my strong ideological commitment to the
resolution or at least the amelioration of this major problem area in
our society. In time, I moved back into the ranks of academia, resum-

ing my more comfortable roles of teacher and researcher immersed in the ethnographic intricacies and theoretical concerns relating to Mesoamerica, North American Indians, and psychological anthropology. Although there have been moments when I was tempted to dismiss those earlier years as mere interludes, I have more often pondered both their value for me and the perplexing problems posed by my attempts at applying anthropology.

I turn now to a consideration of graduate training and its relevance and value for anthropologists who, by choice or by circumstance, function in applied settings. From the above discussion one might be led to conclude that graduate education is superfluous in some respects and wanting in others. As to superfluity, I do not see that we need to be concerned. For acquiring general and basic skills—the sharpening of an inquiring mind, the inculcation of the analytic approach, the organization and communication of research findings—and for gaining a working familiarity with specific concepts and techniques, the doctoral years are unequivocally relevant. Thus in both of the applied milieux in which I worked, I utilized the modes of thinking, questioning, and conceptualizing that are germane to the social sciences generally. For my campus culture studies I drew directly upon anthropological training and in particular upon acculturation and enculturation theory. The fact that I was unable to mount a major or sustained anthropological program during my tenure at the state commission did not diminish my preference for conceptualizing in terms of the dominant role of culture, the subcultures of ethnic, racial, and religious minorities, the nature of culture change, culture contact theory, and so on.

As for the possibility that graduate training might be found wanting, particularly for the incipient applied anthropologist, a variety of shortcomings could be cited for most graduate programs. Many, if not most, anthropologists would probably agree that their formal preparation for a career was noticeably skewed. The overriding emphasis has been, and still is, upon didactic, academic, and scholarly concerns, and as a result there has been but scant training in the actual application of anthropological knowledge. Here under the rubric of "applied" I include the ordeal of fieldwork and the sink-or-swim approach to teaching, student advising, etc., along with the wide range of possibilities that we more commonly associate with applied anthropology, e.g., in medicine, psychology, education, and the like.

The pervasive scholarly and humanistic emphases associated with our profession are consistent with the fact that most departments of anthropology are located by tradition either at a small liberal arts college or in a college of letters and science within the larger university. To date this has probably been fitting and proper. By and large, anthropologists have viewed themselves as scientists, augmenting and consolidating a growing discipline. But it is becoming increasingly evident that the role of scholar has its limitations, deficiencies that can be sharply sensed whenever one moves away from the traditional halls-of-ivy scientist or social scientist model. Even in the idealized college setting, the professor is typically more than an academician. Not only does he wear the mantle of scientist/scholar but his teaching function makes him a practitioner of his profession. Indeed, his involvement in and dedication to this role may well represent the major preference and focus of a lifetime in the discipline. However, as we all know, with rare exception his effectiveness as a teacher has never been bolstered by an iota of formal instruction in the art of teaching. Rather, his success depends upon a combination of personality, cognitive style, and the vagaries of experience.

What has been said regarding the lack of preparation for practicing the art of anthropology in the classroom can be multiplied many times for those positions where application is paramount and scholarly pursuits are secondary. We are now touching upon a critical contemporary issue since, as noted earlier, it is becoming increasingly apparent that anthropology may well move more and more in the direction of professional practice with whatever concomitant changes in training, image, and status that such a development might imply. At this point it may prove enlightening to scan the history of other fields that have experienced a similar metamorphosis of this order. Clinical psychology represents one such example, and we might also look briefly to the science and art of practicing medicine for additional guidelines.

Psychology offers a loose parallel to anthropology inasmuch as during its early history the focus was upon the establishment and development of the academic discipline with those involved functioning almost wholly within the framework of the scientist model. Among subsequent branchings within the field, the case of clinical psychology is perhaps the most instructive for present purposes, although there are other subfields where application is also a primary consideration, e.g., educational or industrial psychology.

Clinical psychologists are, for the most part, committed to the understanding, diagnosis, and treatment of emotional and mental disorders, yet their education has continued to be predicated upon an uneasy compromise between the roles of scholar and practitioner. Although most clinicians seldom actively utilize their science training, Ph.D. programs perpetuate the dual image of scientist and professional by requiring evidence of thoroughgoing and original scholarly research capabilities in course work and an approved thesis. A recent development in clinical psychology may be relevant to our discussion, namely a new degree program, Doctor of Psychology (Psy.D.), that de-emphasizes research and is dedicated chiefly to the development of clinicians through focused didactic and experiential learning.

When we turn to medicine we find, of course, that training traditionally revolves around the practitioner/professional model. A medical student has the option of selecting a career in medical research but the overwhelming emphasis is upon fostering the talents and skills that make the practice of medicine an art. Again, first-hand experience in the form of extensive practice under close supervision is a central feature of the learning process.

Assuming a general shift in the direction of applied anthropology that will cut across all branches of our discipline (which may well be of greater magnitude than any of us realizes), there is reason to speculate on the shape of things to come at the graduate level. It is not impossible to foresee the establishment of professional schools of anthropology bearing a resemblance, at least in a general way, to existing schools of, for example, social work, nursing, medicine, law, or engineering. Presumably a professional school of anthropology would incorporate the holistic, humanistic perspective that is the hallmark of our science with supervised experience in a variety of specialties that represent the areas where anthropology crosscuts the interests of government, medical and biological sciences, community institutions, and so forth. Perhaps such schools would offer a Doctor of Anthropology degree, but whatever the form and title invoked to signify successful completion, this type of training would have the virtue of eradicating, or at least minimizing, the personality split that can grow out of a double identity associated with the scientist/practitioner image that characterizes applied anthropology in its present state.

Closer to possible realization than the semi-autonomous professional school would be the development of a two-track system within existing graduate departments. One progression might follow the academic/research tradition conferring the Ph.D. while the other would concentrate on socially oriented applied training with opportunities for first-hand participation as practicing anthropologists in the larger world and culminating in a specialized professional degree.

Finally, it is also possible to foresee a time (or perhaps it is already upon us!) when there will be a need for anthropological paraprofessionals and technicians functioning in a capacity analogous to that of the physician's assistant, laboratory technician, or occupational therapist. The individual electing this career choice would be well-grounded in the fundamentals of anthropological theory and methodology and, additionally, would undergo intensive specialty training either at the master's or in certain instances at the bachelor's level. Thus we could draw upon the talents and energies of enthusiastic, dedicated, and potentially competent young people for whom a doctoral education might be too taxing whether intellectually, emotionally, financially, or in terms of the time commitment, but who could contribute significantly in a team setting to a wide variety of applied anthropological programs.

REFERENCES

Bushnell, John H., 1959. What Are the Changing Characteristics of the Undergraduate and What Do these Changes Mean for Programs of General Education? In *Current Issues in Higher Education*, Association for Higher Education. (Washington, D.C.: National Education Association), pp. 137-142.
————, 1960. Student Values: A Summary of Research and Future Problems. In *The Larger Learning: Teaching Values to College Students*, Marjorie Carpenter, ed. (Dubuque: Wm. C. Brown), pp. 45-61.
————, 1962. Student Culture at Vassar. In *The American College*, Nevitt Sanford, ed. (New York: Wiley), pp. 489-514.
————, 1964. Student Culture at Vassar. In *College and Character*, Nevitt Sanford, ed. (New York: Wiley), pp. 146-152.

The Nature of "Applied" Physical Anthropology

Louise M. Robbins

To speak of "applied" physical anthropology may introduce questions such as: How can an instructor of academic courses on fossilized hominid fragments or prehistoric skeletons, on primates, or on population genetics apply his or her knowledge to practical problems in contemporary societies? What practical and theoretical concepts are imparted to students in physical anthropology programs that will enable them to seek positions in which they can apply those concepts? How, specifically, does a person apply physical anthropological knowledge? If one were to search through the recent plethora of physical anthropology textbooks, no section on the application of the subject matter would be found; nor would one find sections that clearly identify the concepts, methods, or theories of the field. Nevertheless, there are applied physical anthropologists in academia, industry, government agencies, and occasionally in private practice. Some individuals work full time on applied problems, others work part time on such projects, and still others work in applied areas on a periodic basis.

Before we examine the subject of applied physical anthropology, it is essential that we look at the label *physical anthropologist* and at the people who have that label because this has important bearing on the interpretations of applied activities. A physical anthropologist is not necessarily one who passed through the program of a traditional, or even an innovative, anthropology department. Many individuals who wear the physical anthropology label obtained their degrees in medicine, dentistry, anatomy, zoology, genetics, or physiology, to name some of the well-represented disciplines. (The nontraditional anthropology background is particularly true of physical anthropologists in Europe.) These individuals are nonetheless active, participating members of the American Association of Physical Anthropologists (AAPA), and many of them make positive contributions to the endeavors of that society; for example, T. Dale Stewart (M.D.) and Mildred Trotter (Ph.D. in anatomy) are past presidents of the AAPA. Some physical anthropologists have two degrees, in anthropology and in medicine, dentistry, or some related field. From one point of view, the discipline of physical anthropology itself may be considered an applied field in which individuals with diverse training backgrounds apply their expertise to the study of the biocultural human animal. While the historical development of anthropology in the United States, with its major separation of physical and cultural areas, may have contributed to the diversity of physical anthropologists (that is, physical anthropologists being considered more as biologists or anatomists than as anthropologists because they were often placed in other departments), I believe the overriding contributing factor to the diversity lies in the complexity of the subject being studied—the human animal.

Within the last twenty years or so, more and more physical anthropologists are coming from traditional anthropology departments. (As of this writing between forty to fifty departments now have programs in which a student may emphasize physical anthropology at the Ph.D. level in the United States.) During the training period, however, the student is still exposed to the diversity of physical anthropologists through the literature, professional meetings, and the varied activities of major professors. The application of his or her training is constantly present although, admittedly, it is rarely revealed to the student in explicit terms for reasons that will be clarified later in the paper.

The concept of applied anthropology and what it entails, I believe, is viewed differently by physical anthropologists and sociocultural anthropologists. I want to discuss this statement from two directions: one, how the concept might be interpreted for physical anthropology; and two, how physical anthropologists themselves view the concept.

For most sociocultural anthropologists applied anthropology focuses on the solution of practical problems in the contemporary world usually involving some measure of cultural change. Some sociocultural anthropologists include in the concept of "applied" a formalized client-agent association between the anthropologist and the agency, individual, or whoever hires the specialist. In this vein, then, physical anthropologists hired by dental schools, most particularly in departments of dental anatomy and orthodontia, function as applied anthropologists. Robert Biggerstaff at the University of Kentucky, Stephen

Ward at Washington University in St. Louis, Albert Dahlberg at the University of Chicago, and I at the University of Nebraska have (or had) a client-agent situation in our work to resolve problems of variation in growth and development of facial morphology with respect to dental changes. By the same token, physical anthropologists teaching anatomy in medical schools are applying their knowledge of human variation to the problems of anatomical differences, the task for which they (the agent) were hired (by the client). The list of physical anthropologists who work, or have worked, in applied areas could be expanded to include Stanley Garn's work in growth, development, and physiological variation at the Fels Institute in Ohio and more recently at the University of Michigan; Solomon Katz's work in dental medicine at Pennsylvania University; Ellis Kerley's work at the Air Force Pathological Institute before he re-entered academia; William Maples's (1973) work in a primate center in Africa; Adelaide Bullen's (1956) work for Harvard's Graduate School of Business Administration; and my contract with an archeological team to study prehistoric skeletal populations from sites in Mississippi. Many other examples could be cited, but the point being made is that what may be interpreted as applied work by some anthropologists may be interpreted differently by others.

Some areas of applied physical anthropology are more apparent than others and probably more acceptable to sociocultural anthropologists because the work is outside academia; it involves the solution of practical contemporary problems and it has a client-agent relationship. Problems in forensic anthropology and human engineering provide both intermittent and permanent employment for many physical anthropologists. Since the time of World War II Thomas McKern, Mildred Trotter, T. Dale Stewart, Russell Newman, Albert Damon, and many others have been employed by the military establishment to devise size standards for military wearing apparel and equipment, identify unknown war dead, investigate heat and cold tolerances, and identify air crash victims. With the advent of the aerospace program, physical anthropologists like H. T. E. Hertzberg (1958) and Charles Clauser worked (the lattter still does) with the Human Engineering program at Wright-Patterson Air Base in Dayton, Ohio; Joseph Young and others were employed in the Aerospace Medicine program at Norman, Oklahoma; and during the 1950's and 1960's Georg Neumann at Indiana University lost a number of predoctoral physical anthropology students to aircraft corporations, where they were employed in departments of human engineering and design. From my own experience, students with B.A. degrees opted for employment in industry and government agencies where they could apply their training immediately rather than continue with graduate studies.

Many physical anthropologists in the United States and elsewhere work regularly or periodically on forensic problems.[1] Individuals like Clyde Snow (1973), Ellis Kerley, Sheilagh Brooks, T. Dale Stewart, William Bass, and others assist law enforcement agencies at the local, state, or national level with human identification problems. Most of us, however, work from an academic position, which tends to mask the applied aspects of the job. A report of our analysis and interpretation is made to the hiring agency and further publication of it rarely occurs.

I do not believe that physical anthropologists give much thought to the concept of applied anthropology. I suspect, although I cannot speak for all physical anthropologists, that the concept is viewed as an epiphenomenon of sociocultural anthropology. This does not mean that physical anthropologists ignore, deny, or are unaware of the applied aspects of their work; they simply view it as a part of the diversity that constitutes physical anthropology; no additional label is needed. To illustrate the point, a symposium on applied physical anthropology was held at the annual AAPA meeting in 1947 (Stewart 1948), but the word *applied* appeared in the title of only one paper. In fact, I do not recall an "applied" paper being listed in the program of an AAPA meeting in the last fifteen years, yet numerous papers with applied foci have been presented.[2] For example, a full-day symposium on forensic anthropology is listed in the 1975 AAPA program. (Two "applied" papers also are listed in the 1975 program but to be read by title only, with no oral presentation.)

Two factors seem to be implicit and crucial to the use and acceptance of the term *applied anthropology*. One factor is the semantic interpretation of, and the emphasis on, the term *applied* as conceived by a sociocultural anthropologist, on the one hand, and a physical anthropologist on the other. A second and related factor pertains to *anthropology* or, more succinctly, to *anthropologist*, with all the implications of professionalism through training, research, identity, and so on. The crux of the problem focuses on how far removed from the academic setting and in what job capacities one can function and still retain professional identity, membership, and so forth as an anthropologist. While these questions caused considerable concern and discussion among sociocultural members of the American Anthropological Association Manpower committees, they have little relevance to physical anthropology because of the inherent diversity of the profession, both in and away from academia. So far as I know, these questions have not been discussed at a physical anthropology meeting or in conversation between physical anthropologists.

Many physical anthropologists on university campuses have appointments in two or more departments; their appointments may be for teaching, for research, or for both. During the period of their academic affiliation, they may work, through contract or consultation, on applied projects related to human engineering, stress and disease, nutrition, and so on. They may leave the academic community for a job in private industry or a government agency, and the job may be a permanent relocation, or it may be only for a specified period of time. Nonacademic physical anthropologists maintain links with their colleagues and their profession through correspondence, participation in meetings, and through publication in professional journals. The range of individual training, research, and job diversity is not emphasized, nor is it hidden; it is simply accepted. Attention centers on the work and its contribution to knowledge, or to the solution of problems of humans.

It may be that physical anthropologists are able to work in pure (if there is such a thing) or applied areas with equal ease, and with little thought of distinguishing the two areas, for several reasons. First, theoretical concepts and various analytical methods and techniques are an integral part of course instruction as a student moves through studies of bones, primates, genetics, and, as is frequently the case, courses in biological and natural sciences, so that a particular (flexible) perspective is acquired for studying biocultural relationships. Second, many physical anthropology students who graduate from traditional departments receive as much, if not more, training in areas of cultural anthropology, which augments their perspective on the biocultural nature of human populations. Third, physical anthropologists are less concerned with the label *applied* than with the work they are doing. Hence, my work with law enforcement agencies, private museums, county dental societies, and contract archeologists is applied anthropology, as is the work of a former student in the design department of a private corporation, but I never think of specifying it as such.

Problems arise that need to be resolved. I, my colleagues, and the students we train have expertise that may help to resolve those problems. We work toward that end.

NOTES

[1]Physical anthropology is one of nine sections in the American Academy of Forensic Sciences. The academy promotes the interdisciplinary study and research of medicolegal problems related to human identification.

[2]For a list of articles published in the *American Journal of Physical Anthropology* on applied physical anthropology see Levine (1971).

REFERENCES

Bullen, Adelaide K., 1956. *New Answers to the Fatigue Problem* (Gainesville: University of Florida Press).

Hertzberg. H. T. E., ed., 1958. *Annotated Bibliography of Applied Physical Anthropology in Human Engineering*, WADC Technical Report 56-30 (Wright-Patterson Air Force Base, Dayton, Ohio: Wright Air Development Command).

Levine, Morton H., 1971. *A Topical Guide to Volumes 1-21 (New Series)*, *American Journal of Physical Anthropology* (Philadelphia: Wistar Institute Press).

Maples, William R., 1973. The Physical Anthropologist in Primate Research Facilities in Africa. In *Anthropology Beyond the University*, Alden Redfield, ed., Southern Anthropological Society Proceedings, No. 7 (Athens: University of Georgia Press), pp. 18-25.

Snow, Clyde C., 1973. Forensic Anthropology. In *Anthropology Beyond the University*, Alden Redfield, ed., Southern Anthropological Society Proceedings, No. 7 (Athens: University of Georgia Press), pp. 4-17.

Stewart, T. Dale, ed., 1948. Symposium on Applied Physical Anthropology. *American Journal of Physical Anthropology* 6 (3):315-380.

Conflict and Planned Change in the Development of Community Health Services

Lucy M. Cohen

The planning of community health services emerges as one of the recent revolutions in the United States. As public responsibility has extended to the medical sectors, social scientists have been called upon to assess the complex dimensions involved in redirecting our systems of health care. Although the concept of planning has developed to sizable proportions in the health fields, limited attention has been given to the conflicts inherent in the planning process. Major biomedical innovations have made possible new and more effective ways of coping with illness, but gaps exist between new knowledge and its implementation by care-givers. With the increased coordination of the medical world, provider and consumer groups have been called upon to adopt new values and regulations designed to govern their relations with each other. This paper draws on two cases to illustrate the conflicts and accommodations faced by participants in major innovative programs. Data about the first community mental health center in Washington, D.C., will be complemented by material drawn from the evaluation of the development of a neighborhood health center in a major Southern city.[1]

Increasingly, planning models are being incorporated into public policy in health. Grand designs are juxtaposed with models that attempt to represent the specific interests of a region, a state, or a local community. Words such as *needs, goals, objectives, processes,* and *evaluation* have become part of the plans generated by health care administrators (Myrdal 1960; Rosenfeld 1968). Although to some of us planning means preparing designs and projects called for by a funding agency, planning can also be viewed as a dynamic process directed toward adaptation to changing circumstances in communities

(Spiegel 1968). Its central role in the evolution of health care calls for identifying critical issues that emerge from the anticipated and unanticipated consequences of change.

The recent passage of the National Health Planning and Resources Development Act of 1974[2] challenges anthropologists to examine ways through which the discipline can contribute to the concerns associated with such major pieces of national legislation. As planning moves to a central position in the field of health care, we should examine the types of conflicts and patterns of conflict resolution which accompany innovations in rapidly changing health care systems. Study of local agencies can serve as focal points for understanding critical issues involved in planning for proposed change.

The case of the community mental health center program in Washington, D.C., points to problems stemming from our piecemeal system of planning, a system that makes it difficult to implement fully the objectives of national legislation and policy at local program levels. The health department in this case reorganized in response to the national call for new directions in the delivery of mental health services. But changes resulting from competing federal legislation created roadblocks to the full attainment of any single set of objectives. Under continuous demands for change, individual programs tenaciously maintained solidarity and continuity. But such unity is actually a defense against the constant demands for reorganization. As such, it has been counterproductive for the legislative goals of reconceptualizing mental health care.

The second illustration highlights the tensions that have characterized efforts to redistribute decision-making authority and accountability in the neighborhood-based health services network of a Southern city. As consumers have assumed responsibility for identifying their health care needs and services, they have entered into new relationships with major interest groups in their community and with representatives of national health care organizations. Shifts have occurred in the balance of power of these groups, resulting in nebulously defined areas of decision-making. The norms and sanctions that govern accountability for the moral and technical order in the new primary care centers have become increasingly difficult to identify.

Interlocking circumstances influenced the development of the Area C Community Mental Health Center in Washington, D.C. Throughout the 1940's and 1950's a growing body of literature linked mental illness to conditions in the sociocultural environment and recommended early intervention in the crises of individuals to retard future disability. The momentum for the growth of the community psychiatry movement of this period came also from the development of new psychotropic drugs enabling state hospitals to discharge long-term patients and to improve prognosis for new patients. The resulting legislative activity culminated in 1963 with the first presidential message ever sent to Congress in support of mental health programs (Cohen 1971). In that same year Congress enacted PL 88-164, the Kennedy-sponsored Mental Retardation Facilities and Community Mental Health Centers Construction Act of 1963. Regulations were issued in May 1964 which specified the "essential" and "adequate" elements needed to provide appropriate care.[3]

The Department of Public Health of the District of Columbia, along with other major mental health facilities in the country, responded to this federal stimulus for the expansion of community mental health services. Interest in the program was spurred in particular by President Kennedy's special message that the District of Columbia should serve as a model for the nation in important areas of human service. A mental health planner and staff were hired to hasten the development of community mental health services. One of the early planning activities was to help identify community needs for mental health centers, following the patterns suggested by the new federal legislation. On the basis of figures regarding use of publicly supported mental health services and other demographic data, Health Service "Area C" was selected for development of the first comprehensive program of mental health services in the city. This was a catchment area of 250,000 people, with a predominately black population. Area C represented the poorest people in the city and the least educated.[4] A large portion of the area's population relied on public facilities for health services. Surveys of the time disclosed graphically the gaps in professional mental health personnel. Only two psychiatrists had a private practice in the area, contrasted with the 120 in the most affluent sector of the city (Government of the District of Columbia 1965).

The city Health Department applied for a federal demonstration grant for its first community mental health center in 1964. The National Institute of Mental Health approved the grant with one stipulation, that the director of Area C would have to be selected with federal approval (El-Hehiawy 1971).

The 1965 demonstration grant provided for administrative and program support. Special emergency and community-based mental health services were to extend concepts of prevention. Programs for adults, children, adolescents, the aged, alcoholics, and drug addicts were to be developed and strengthened. A program evaluation and research section was to regularly review and interpret the center's activities.

By 1968 new modifications in the administrative structure of the city Department of Public Health took place as a result of federal comprehensive health planning legislation. Joint community health and mental health systems were now emphasized with a three-level system of service. The neighborhood health center was to serve for primary care, supported by intermediate and specialized health facilities. Consequently, mental health was restructured as a tri-level system to be fused within the medically oriented community health program.

Area C participated in this tri-level system until 1970, when two other major reorganizations in the system of services of the city called for alterations in the concepts underlying the community mental health programs. First, the city followed the trend in other parts of the country to bring together under a single administrative umbrella the major human and social services of the city, such as health, public welfare, veterans' affairs, and vocational rehabilitation. Second, under the stimulus of federal legislation, the city authorities established a new administration for the treatment of drug addicts. Structural changes occurred once again in mental health services, as new lines of authority and responsibility were drawn.

Thus, within a period of five years, from 1965 to 1970, planning at Area C experienced frequent calls for shifts and alterations caused by new directions in mental health care and human services at national and local levels. One consequence of these changes was an increase in the turnover of the center directors. Each policy change and new administration confronted the staff with modifications and new instructions. As a result, staff within individual units and programs found it difficult to join together to develop commonly shared ideas, policies, and missions (El-Hehiawy 1971). The center functioned with a set of loosely joined units lacking a strong, unified sense of directed and shared values. Single programs, such as those of the geriatric or adolescent units, achieved solidarity, but although such solidarity contributed to the continuity of the center as a whole, it frustrated the objectives of coordinated development and change. Unit autonomy, nevertheless, functioned as an adaptive response to change and shifts in center leadership.

These highlights simplify events that were admittedly much more complex. I would like to complement these materials with case data that draw attention to the dilemmas involved in delineating boundaries of authority and accountability in primary care centers as consumer groups attempt to enter the arenas of power and influence in health care organizations.

Neighborhood health center legislation emphasized participation of the populations served, both as policy-makers and as employees (Schorr and English 1968). Its aim was to develop accessible and high-quality comprehensive health services for low-income populations. Neighborhood health center projects introduced a number of new dimensions to the ambulatory health center movement, such as the management of complex, nonacademic, service-oriented projects; consumer participation in decision-making; and political and social conflicts arising from federal, state, and poor communities' efforts to influence the operation of health services heretofore under the control of health departments, physicians, and hospitals (Merten and Nothman 1975).

In their evaluation of the early development of a neighborhood health center in a major Southern city, New et al. (1973) point to the contrasting aspirations of professionals and the citizenry. A group of black leaders in a neighborhood of a Southern city organized to consider community problems. They established a health committee to identify mental health needs. As a result of their deliberations they decided to request $13,000 to establish a half-way house for alcoholics and other former patients of a state hospital who had nowhere to go after they left the institution. The health committee sent the proposal to Washington. It was not funded, but another federal agency suggested that there were now larger sums of money available to start comprehensive health programs. Consequently, the local medical school received millions to establish a health center in that neighborhood.

Concurrent events contributed to the evolution of the center. A federal government official approached the local medical school to inquire about its interest in establishing a neighborhood health center. The dean of the medical school asked for time to plan, as no one on his faculty knew much about the operation of such an organization.

At the same time, members of the local white medical society who were thinking of starting a fee-for-service health center had done some planning. Eventually they agreed that the medical school would be the appropriate sponsor of the neighborhood project. A former member of the medical school's board of trustees convinced the dean that he should submit an application to the federal agency. Two months before the deadline, several medical school and medical society personnel visited other existing health centers in the country and quickly wrote a proposal.

Although the medical school faculty preferred establishing the center in one location, the local poverty agency had already designated another area, and the school went along with this plan. Relatively little attention was paid to the leaders and citizens of the community, particularly to the role they would play as members of the policy board of the health center, as stipulated by the federal agency.

After the grant was approved, the black medical association in that city, already critical of the policies of the medical school and its affiliated hospitals, complained that it had not been consulted about a project director. After a series of meetings with all the groups, a black physician agreeable to all the parties was selected. He was made project co-director.

Different interests and values have shaped the early directions of the center. Views conflicted about the functions of citizens on the board. Do consumers serve in an advisory or policy-making capacity? How are the boundaries of influence to be delineated over matters relating to technical competence and general operating procedures? How are priorities to be established when the federal government sees the center as a demonstration project, the medical school defines it as a training and research setting, and the community as a place for health care and employment?

New et al. suggest that as it is now constituted, the health center carries out citizen participation in an adversary type of relationship. There is little joint effort among professionals, consumers, and decision-makers. Each group wants to assume control, but each holds the others accountable for problems that arise. The citizens remember that they attempted to establish a $13,000 half-way house to help members of the community. Before this could be achieved, another group from a "segregationist" school took over the project to create a much larger structure which the citizens could not control. Conflicts of interest abound and the citizens hold the health service providers accountable for some of the problems created.

Delineating the boundaries of accountability has then become a central issue in operating the center. Each group perceives different functions and competencies for such a facility. Contrasting views are accentuated by the presence of various institutions: the sponsoring medical school, the community, the local poverty agency, the county medical society (white), the medical association (black), and the federal funding agency. The policy-makers must determine the directions and set the responsibilities of the center against this complex background.

As anthropologists preparing to participate in the new health planning and resource development, we should bring perspectives derived from our cumulative assessment of newly emerging policies and programs. The two cases highlighted in this paper offer examples of the types of conflicts that occur as members of health organizations and interest groups become involved in reconceptualization and reorganization. The illustrations represent efforts undertaken in response to major mental health and health care legislation. While the pioneering legislation reflects innovative conceptual and programmatic models, the fragmented nature of plans and policy has resulted in contradictory and unsystematic changes.

The case of Area C concerned the fate of operating unit staff members who bore the responsibility of responding to each new plan. Program personnel did not have the option of openly rejecting reforms approved by higher echelons. The changed guidelines to action which emerged from diverse authorities confronted these health care providers with challenging readjustments. Overwhelmed by this continuous flow of information, administrators—who could have become the links between old and new forms of mental health care—became the highest "at risk" categories. Area C experienced serious difficulties with the selection and retention of administrators, notwithstanding the federal agency's participation in the choice of center directors. The absence of a unifying and directing force strengthened the solidarity of members within individual programs. This contributed to the maintenance of the center itself, but the original mental health plan envisioned by President Kennedy has not been fulfilled.

The case of the neighborhood health center documents controversies facing educational institutions when they are forced into new power-sharing relationships with populations traditionally viewed only as the recipients of service. The representatives of the medical school who participated in the early plans for the center acknowledged limited awareness of the concepts to which the program would commit them. Yet the university dean, who had hoped for time to plan and to learn about this new type of organization, decided to bypass that phase under the influence of interest groups and the pressures of the federal funding agency itself.

The consumers, whose original request for a half-way house was submerged in the process of delineating power and responsibilities in the new center, became marginal participants in the movement to extend new services into their neighborhood. The case demonstrates how representatives of federal organizations authorized to create local interest in a project may continue to support the authority and power of traditional providers of public health services to poverty areas. The contraditictions which result from plans to redelegate power need serious examination.

Research into the processes of planned change in these contexts draws our attention to the accommodations demanded by increased commitment to planning and rapid development. With the health agencies and systems being called upon increasingly to become key agents of change, they become prime subjects for comparative studies of political and social relations. The responses of local communities or regions to national movements for restructuring health services reflect coalitions of major interest groups. They represent shared as well as contrasting visions of medical priorities and problems, and diverse expectations regarding the distribution of resources and power. Interpretations of statutes and guidelines may be influenced by professionals, consumers, legislators, or researchers. Identifying the forms of dispute and conflict settlement followed by these groups should offer information about the crises arising in the administration of human service agencies.

Anthropologists with specific interest in the relation of law to custom within health care organizations should trace the evolution of plans and statutes before and after implementation. Steele and Deasy (1973) directed such research in a study on legislative change and rural/urban mental health service delivery systems in northwest Florida. In their work on the impact of the Florida Mental Health Act (Baker Act) in an eight-county area, these authors documented the tendency for "gatekeepers" such as sheriffs, judges, public health nurses, and mental health workers to view the act as "unrealistic" and of "potential detriment to the status of mental health care in the entire catchment area" (Steele and Deasy 1973:15).

As applied anthropologists, we must attend to the social and cultural dynamics governing the reactions of care-givers to the constant flow of new knowledge and plans. Brody (1975) recently pointed to the sharp cultural impact of rapidly changing biomedical knowledge and technique in the fields of medicine. The gathering philosophical and value crisis in the medical worlds deserves serious consideration from students of culture. The anthropologist is a natural participant observer in a variety of medical and health settings, including "acute decision-making arenas as well as ethics and human volunteer committees and other emerging groups" (Brody 1975:25).

Major health planning legislation in our own country and abroad should lead to collaboration among anthropologists in researching these relatively little-understood medical arenas. Participation in endeavors involving legislation and policy development can draw on concepts from the study of government, law, and social conflict. Preparing applied anthropologists to move in these new directions will require innovative training programs.

In recent years, an increasing number of departments have established new applied anthropology programs at the M.A. and Ph.D. levels. Expansion of fieldwork training requires experiences that will prepare students for work in agencies and communities such as the ones described in this paper. Two aspects of this field training should receive special attention: the need for collaborative research endeavors between universities and agencies, and the expansion of continuing education programs in anthropology among members of the health professions.

As yet relatively few anthropologists are employed in health agencies or community programs. In these settings they could provide educational guidance for students engaged in fieldwork. While I was on the staff of the Area C Center, we collaborated with a local university in one of our research endeavors. This involved the university project director, twelve students, and three agency staff members. As chief of program evaluation of the center, I had a major role in selecting the research problem.

The project was conducted during the changing and tension-ridden periods described earlier in this paper. During the year in which we completed the report for publication, major city and agency reorganizations took place. The final manuscript was reviewed by local agency personnel, researchers, and representatives of old and new administrations. Without the benefit of coordination between qualified representatives of the agency and the university, the project could not have been brought to completion. Students worked successfully during crises and under strained circumstances—conditions characteristic of a number of public government systems in our country.

A final important aspect relates to the expansion of continuing education programs. Anthropologists now are well-established on the faculties of medical, public health, nursing, and other professional schools. But our discipline has played a limited role, thus far, in continuing education projects, or in postgraduate programs. This is unfortunate because contemporary education in medicine stresses continuing training to update knowledge and skills and to insure the expansion of needed basic research.

We should explore ways through which to participate in these efforts. In the past few years I have undertaken on-the-job consultation with health practitioners and with directors of in-service training programs interested in the interfaces of cultural and behavioral factors. I meet with faculty involved in the advanced education of nurses and social workers and with physicians who wish to incorporate anthropological findings in their research.

Some years ago Alexander Leighton (1946) underscored the benefits for research and practice to be derived from working in the field or the clinical setting. The cases discussed here corroborate the wisdom of research and educational endeavors in the settings where health action programs take place. Anthropologists who cooperate directly in planning and implementing applied programs have unique opportunities to advance our understanding of society and of human behavior. In the settings where plans are implemented and practice takes place they can observe and test the ways through which planned change shapes the lives of individuals and groups.

NOTES

[1]Cases were drawn from three sources: Cohen (1971), El-Hehiawy (1971), and New, Hessler, and Cater (1973). The author gratefully acknowledges her indebtedness to Mrs. El-Hehiawy and Dr. New for permission to use their materials in this paper.

[2]Public Law 93-641, 93rd Congress, January 4, 1975.

[3]The five essential elements included in-patient care, out-patient care, partial hospitalization, emergency care, and consultation and education; it included also the components of diagnostic service, rehabilitation service, precare and aftercare, training and research, and evaluation (Smith and Hobbs 1966).

[4]31.3 percent of this group had less than a $4,000 income in 1959; 24.5 percent had less than an eighth-grade education (Government of the District of Columbia 1965; El-Hehiawy 1971).

REFERENCES

Brody, Eugene B., 1975. Rights, Privileges and Obligations: The Physician as Bioethicist. In *Anthrolopogy and Society*, Bela C. Maday, ed. (Washington: Anthropological Society of Washington), pp. 18-26.

Cohen, Lucy M., 1971. The Community Mental Health Movement. In *Patients in Programs at Area C Community Mental Health Center*, Lucy M. Cohen, Leila Calhoun Deasy, Nancy P. El-Hehiawy, and Jirina Polivka, eds. (Washington, D.C.: Department of Human Resources), pp. 3-16.

El-Hehiawy, Nancy, 1971. The Development of the Area C Community Mental Health Center: A Case Study in Social Change. In *Patients in Programs at Area C Community Mental Health Center*, Lucy M. Cohen, Leila Calhoun Deasy, Nancy P. El-Hehiawy, and Jirina Polivka, eds. (Washington, D.C.: Department of Human Resources), pp. 17-38.

Government of the District of Columbia Department of Public Health, 1965. *Comprehensive Mental Health Services in the District of Columbia* (Washington, D.C.: Government of the District of Columbia Department of Public Health).

Leighton, Alexander H., 1946. "Applied" Research and "Pure" Research. *American Anthropologist* 48:667-668.

Merten, Walter, and Sylvia Nothman, 1975. Neighborhood Health Center Experience. *American Journal of Public Health* 65:248-252.

Myrdal, Gunnar, 1960. *Beyond the Welfare State* (New Haven: Yale University Press).

New, Peter K., R. Hessler, and P. B. Cater, 1973. Consumer Control and Public Accountability. *Anthropological Quarterly* 46:196-213.

Rosenfeld, Leonard S., 1968. Problems in Planning Community Health Services. *Bulletin of the New York Academy of Medicine* 44:166-185.

Schorr, Lisbeth Bamberger, and Joseph T. English, 1968. Background, Context and Significant Issues in Neighborhood Health Center Programs. *The Milbank Memorial Fund Quarterly* 46:289-296.

Smith, M. Brewster, and Nicholas Hobbs, 1966. *The Community and the Community Mental Health Center* (Washington: American Psychological Association).

Spiegel, Hans B. C., 1968. Health Planning in the Context of Comprehensive Community Development. *Bulletin of the New York Academy of Medicine* 44:199-203.

Steele, Carolyn I., and Leila Calhoun Deasy, 1973. *Changes in Florida's Mental Health Legislation: Perspectives of Deliverers of Services in Rural Areas.* (Paper read at the National Conference on Social Welfare, Atlantic City, N.J.)

Anthropology in the Urban Planning Process: A Review and an Agenda

ROBERT M. WULFF

APPLIED anthropologists, particularly those specializing in urban problems, are continually asking themselves: "Must we abandon anthropology to be useful outside academe"? As a result of my particular interests and experiences,[1] I have been confronted by a specific variation on this question: "Can an anthropologist successfully function in urban planning and still retain his identity?" This paper develops a three-part discussion answering the question with qualified affirmation. The paper begins by contrasting the present deficiencies of American urban planning with complementary strengths of anthropology. Second, it presents a state-of-the-art review of anthropological research that has been successfully applied to urban planning. The paper concludes with six specific recommendations for adapting traditional applied anthropology to the requirements of urban problem-solving.

Planning, defined generally as "activity centrally concerned with the linkage between knowledge and organized action" (Friedmann and Hudson 1974:2), has been practiced for quite some time. Urban planning, on the other hand, has been practiced in this country for a relatively short period of time, having only become a recognized profession since the 1920's. Its subsequent developments are important for understanding planning's current problems and anthropology's potential solutions.[2]

From the beginning, the American urban planning profession was dominated by engineers, architects, and economists, and the initial direction and character of urban planning was set by their intellectual interests and training. The majority of these planners were physical determinists, who believed the good life could be created through good physical design. For example, paying little attention to behavioral science data, they attempted to solve urban problems like poverty and crime through the design of sound and aesthetically pleasing housing. Furthermore, their perception and evaluation of the quality of urban life was measured predominantly through economic indicators, with the effect that those measures of life that were merely the easiest to observe were transformed into the most important. The accuracy of this economic data became more important than the significance.

The principal guidance tool was the "comprehensive plan," which attempted to plot a city's long-range goals. The goals were invariably expressed in physical terms (e.g., land use) and thus rarely confronted urban issues such as resource allocation and race. The comprehensive plan all but disregarded urban subcultural variations. It assumed social homogeneity and described the city with massive averages. The formula was the same everywhere: "Mix a little bit of amenity, a dash of open space, and some new housing units; tie them together with rapid transit, lots of color, and data . . ." (Kaplan 1974:45).

Finally, and perhaps most damaging of all, the dominant approach to guidance was elitist, top-down planning. Planners took their example from the father of modern public administration, Jeremy Bentham, who boasted he could rule colonial India without ever leaving his London apartment. The majority of urban planners felt a utopian mandate that excluded the opinions and attitudes of the city's residents as valuable contributions to the decision-making process.

Within the last fifteen years the planning profession has encountered numerous urban problems for which its intellectual capacities have been demonstrably inadequate. Awakened by these failures and criticism from within the profession (e.g., Faber and Seers 1972; Kaplan 1974; Friedman 1973a; Goodman 1972), the idea and practice of urban planning have begun to change radically. Five of these changes are of interest to anthropologists: (1) a redirection of existing planning processes away from long-range comprehensive plans to incremental plans dealing with small functionally bound areas; (2) a broadening of the data and interest base to include social indicators, and social planning to deal with the delivery and evaluation of human services; (3) an effort to improve the impact of urban design through a more sophisticated understanding of the relationship between the built environment and urban behavior; (4) an increased sensitivity to the existence and viability of diverse urban lifestyles and the need to consider their varying goals and needs; and (5) a recognition that people should be planned *with* rather than *for* and that citizen participation is valuable for decision-making.

If planners are to succeed in these reforms they will require social science skills. Each of the trends thus represents a point of entry for the anthropologist desiring to apply his expertise to the urban planning process. It is an opportunity our discipline is capable of exploiting, for anthropology's traditional strengths complement urban planning's traditional deficiencies. In particular, our contribution to urban planning will derive from applying anthropology's unique perspective and fieldwork orientation. The general value of these two attributes for understanding contemporary problems has been discussed at length by others (Plotnicov 1974; Foster 1969:56-71; Peattie 1975; Downs 1975; Kessler 1974). Thus, I shall only provide a brief overview of their problem-solving capabilities to set the stage for the detailed review of their specific value for urban planning.

Improved urban planning can come only by creating new perspectives and choices. The cross-cultural and comparative perspective of anthropology can function to this end by enriching the planning solution pool. The removal of urban planning's cultural (and subcultural) blinders can generate a broader awareness of alternate strategies for meeting human needs. The anthropological perspective can also create new choices by redefining the character of old problems. The anthropologist's facility for discovering different views of reality will hasten the breakdown of ethnocentric and time-bound worldviews in which contemporary conditions are mistaken for eternal truths.

Ethnographic fieldwork has long been the hallmark of anthropology. The strengths of this data collection method lie in its open-ended structure and commitment to the insider's view. These strengths can be assets in describing and understanding the urban as well as peasant and primitive societies. In urban planning, where intervening variables are infinite and rarely predictable, the serendipitous quality of fieldwork can be highly advantageous for generating hypotheses and discovering important questions—as opposed to simply producing answers. At a descriptive level the anthropologist can function as an emic "visualizer" (Gulick 1963) of the urban scene. Our traditional participant-observer role provides rich and qualitative pictures of urban behavior from the native point of view.

There is currently no sustained effort on the part of anthropologists to apply their expertise to urban planning. Nor is there any organized attempt by urban planners to recruit anthropologists. Nevertheless, a number of scholars (not all of them anthropologists) have utilized anthropological perspectives and methods to investigate urban planning problems. The following review of the literature is heuristically organized according to four significant problem areas in the field of urban planning: planning theory, planning and pluralism, urban design, and program evaluation.

Planning theory. Urban planning in this country—particularly its social arm—has been exercised largely as a series of responses to crisis situations, which has left little time for planners to assess the validity of their guiding theories of human society and behavior. As a result, innovative theory that derives from self-examination of ends and means has come mainly from researchers outside the planning profession. Among social scientists, anthropologists' contributions to social theory relevant to planning have been significant. Anthropology has functioned as a correcting force questioning the assumptions and definitions concerning the nature of urban society and urban problems commonly held by planners and policy-makers.

Most notable in this respect are the works of Gans (1962), Liebow (1967), Peattie (1968), Bott (1957), Valentine (1966), and Lewis (1966), which have profoundly altered thinking concerning a variety of key policy issues: the social function of "slums," minority unemployment motivations, the content of the planning process, the structure of family services, and the causes of poverty. In addition, I am confident the recent research of Stack (1974), Suttles (1972), Rainwater (1970), and Hannerz (1969) will in the near future similarly reorient urban social intervention strategies.

Planning and pluralism. Planning for the plural city requires detailed knowledge of intra-urban lifestyle variation. Anthropologists, employing the subculture concept and ethnographic methods, have produced insightful analyses of the social units that compose the plural city (Waddell and Watson 1971; Valentine 1974; Johnson and Sanday 1971; J. Jacobs 1974; Gulick 1973:1012-1018; Partridge 1973). While such anthropological studies have provided planners with valuable in-depth descriptions of urban subcultures, those data have been of limited use for solving the basic planning problem: how to identify and measure the diverse needs of these urban communities. However, Jones's (1974) pioneering study of San Diego County provides planners with an excellent working model for overcoming these limitations. Utilizing participant-observation and other ethnographic techniques, Jones is able to isolate meaningful urban social units as well as identify their needs through emic indicators.

Pluralistic planning has recently been transformed into participatory planning as a result of federal legislation that requires community participation in the planning process. Although many sophisticated techniques have been developed to organize and elicit community participation (charette, delphi, decision trees, and mixed scanning), participatory planning has rarely been successful. Participatory planning is a terribly difficult process to institute and maintain; and the blame for its dismal record to date must be laid to both the planners and the community. Nevertheless, one important reason for the failure has been the planners' consistent inability to establish working relationships with the city's subcultural groups. Whether labeled "outreach aides" (by mental health and social service agencies) or "community planners" (by planning departments), few of these representatives of the bureaucracy have achieved rapport with their citizen constituents. However, where anthropological fieldwork methods have been employed to create a long-term intense relationship between change agent and change recipient, participatory planning has worked to define (and occasionally meet) community needs (Grigsby and Campbell 1974; Schensul 1973; S. Jacobs 1974).

Urban Design. Architects of the city's built environment—in both the public and private sectors—are now seriously considering the behavioral needs and design preferences of the user. Unfortunately, design professionals, as representatives of a subculture distinct from their clients, have found it difficult to create user-oriented buildings, parks, houses, and communities (Llewelyn-Davies 1975). Behavioral scientists have demonstrated superior preparation for this task and now conduct the majority of user studies. Because ethnographic studies are ideally suited to the requirements of built environment research, anthropologists have been among the pioneers in this research area. Rapoport's man-environment studies (1971) and Hall's proxemic research (1966) awakened the design professions to the diverse and latent functions of space. Building on this sound base, subsequent anthropologists have investigated the symbolic and behavioral correlates of the built environment and have influenced urban design policy.

For example: anthropologists have proven to be particularly skillful at identifying housing design preferences cross-culturally (Wulff 1973; Rainwater 1966; Esber 1972; and Rapoport 1973); ethnographic research of New York street and apartment life has led to pedestrian-oriented improvements in zoning and street furniture design and the development of crime-deterrant housing design (Braybrooke 1974; Newman 1972): and participant-observation has been utilized to identify the conflicting spatial requirements of staff, clients, and administrators in school and hospital buildings (Sommer 1969).

Program Evaluation. As the indicators of urban social malaise continue to rise, a wide range of helping and public service agencies have begun to re-evaluate their intervention methods and theories. One of the most successful new approaches involves developing social service delivery systems keyed to the recipients' own perceived needs and goals rather than to the values of middle-class professionals. Such programs are best evaluated from the clients' point of view rather than from the administrators' (the latter involving such criteria as intake "body counts" and pre- and post-interviews). Anthropological methods and perspectives are appropriate to this approach; consequently, a variety of excellent client-oriented evaluation studies have been conducted in schools (Ogbu 1974; Rosenfeld 1971; Everhart 1975), the Bureau of Indian Affairs Relocation Program (Snyder 1973), job-training programs (Wellman 1968; Padfield and Williams 1973), welfare service demand (Matthiasson 1974), and hospital services (Shiloh 1966). Important evaluation research has also been conducted by reversing the focus of the ethnographer. That is, the anthropologist can usefully study not only the clients of planning but the process and planners as well (e.g., see Stanton 1970; Selznick 1949; Wolcott 1973; Zimmerman 1974; Carlos and Brokensha 1972; Needleman and Needleman 1974).

A similar insider approach has been successfully applied to evaluation research on a variety of roles within the urban criminal justice system. For exampe, participant-observation research conducted on policemen (Rubinstein 1973; Kelling et al. 1974), prison guards (Jacobs and Retsky 1975), and prisoners (Davidson 1974) has yielded insights into the inconsistencies between the ideal and real workings of the criminal justice system. Ethnographic methods have been particularly valuable for gathering descriptive data on criminal behavior on the street, for it is an arena of human activity completely closed to other research methods commonly used by social scientists (Denfield 1974; Weppner 1973). These unique emic data can be utilized to generate innovative control strategies: Yin's (1972) research on false alarms and fire hydrant abuse and Spradley's (1973) work on public drunkenness sentencing procedures.

The treatment of urban deviance has also been enriched by anthropological research. In problem areas like mental health and juvenile delinquency, many welfare workers and therapists have shifted from intensive individual therapy and casework methods to group treatment techniques. These techniques borrow heavily from anthropology's structural-functional models of extended kin groups and personal networks (e.g., see Attneave and Speck 1974; Leichter and Mitchell 1967).

The preceding review demonstrates the value of anthropology for the practice of urban planning. But the works cited amount to only a timid beginning. The potentials for expanding our efforts in the planning fields are impressive, yet in any such endeavor the discipline will be confronted by challenge as well as opportunity, for anthropology does not come to the tasks of urban planning completely provisioned.

The historical development of applied anthropology in this country has left us unprepared to utilize maximally our unique strengths for the planning of our own cities. With the exception of isolated work among American Indians (e.g., Tax 1958; Lurie 1955) and a highly concentrated research effort during World War II, applied anthropology has been practiced almost exclusively in the developing world where problems of technological impact (Foster 1969), agricultural development (Spicer 1952), native administration (Barnett 1956), and health care innovation (Paul 1955) have been the overriding research interests.

In reviewing the contributions of applied anthropology in 1955, Margaret Mead (1956:95) noted the imbalanced interest in the fate of indigenous non-Western peoples and the concomitant lack of interest in problems entirely internal to Western culture like urbanism, industrial relations, race, and social work. Although certain problems in our own society have become recent concerns in applied anthropology (Weaver 1973), Mead's observation still holds true today, twenty years later.[3]

While today's applied urban anthropologists might still read these earlier works with profit, they are of limited value as models for working in contemporary American cities. Thus, in order to advance from our present precarious toe-hold on the city, we must be prepared to make adaptations in our traditional perspectives and methods. I have stressed above that anthropologists can contribute meaningfully to the urban planning process as anthropologists; and I am convinced that nothing so drastic as "reinventing anthropology" will be necessary to be successful in this new endeavor.[4] Rather, the adaption will require only alteration of our "old" suit: widening the lapels, lengthening the trousers, and taking in the waist. The following six prescriptions are offered as an agenda to guide the tailors among us.

1. *We must discard two traditional but anachronistic concepts.* Cultural relativism and the ideal of value-free social science are two

closely related concepts that will only inhibit the effectiveness of an applied urban anthropologist. The scientific attitude involves a willingness to be objective, but many anthropologists have assumed, additionally, that such willingness implies being completely value-free. The impossibility of such a stance has been noted by intervention-oriented social scientists from Marx (1927) in 1847 to Myrdal (1958). In truth, scientific research is value-saturated. At every step the investigator must choose between competing models, research designs, and measuring instruments. That choice will ultimately reduce to ideology. To properly plan urban change we must admit and understand our own ideologies lest we simply replicate models of our own experience and taste.

We must also abandon the shackles of cultural relativism—the premise that cultures are not to be comparatively evaluated—which has long inhibited the discipline's development of a normative science of culture. Unfortunately, cultural relativism has often been linked with functionalism in anthropological analysis (Kaplan and Manners 1972:37). These two concepts can and must be separated, for I am not suggesting that we also discard functionalism.

Many applied anthropologists have already implicitly discarded the concepts of relativism and a value-free social science. But the time has arrived to explicitly state and support the consequences. In terms of both research and student training, this will mean embracing a problem-solving ethic. This ethic will be perfected and institutionalized as we evolve from a learned society to a profession. As distasteful as the prospect may seem, it appears to be our only realistic path if the histories of the successful applied sciences (e.g., law, medicine, and engineering) are apt lessons. However we need not simply mimic the models of other professions; a number of professionalization scenarios of our own exist (Spicer and Downing 1974:4-6).

2. *We must begin a new period of eclecticism.* Ideologically, this should not be difficult for anthropologists, who have traditionally incorporated ideas from outside the discipline when confronted by new subjects. With respect to urban problem-solving, a number of sister disciplines have valuable seniority, and their important methods and theories must be added to our applied urban tool kit. A minimal list of additions would include: factorial ecology (Berry 1966), time-budget analysis (Chapin 1974), community power theory (Wilson 1968), urban ecology (Theodorson 1961; Bourne 1971), social policy design (Gans 1971), organizational sociology (Argyris 1974), and regional science (Hansen 1972).[5]

3. *We must devise new advice formats.* Our traditional reporting styles and vehicles (e.g., monographs, journal articles, and conference papers) will not enable an applied urban anthropologist to communicate adequately with the majority of his data consumers—whether they be governmental agencies or grass-roots community groups. The problem is simply that advice presented via these standard formats will either be unintelligible or useless to the client.

For example, to provide useful advice to a municipal planning department, in presenting his data the anthropologist will have to become sensitive to the realities of the political decision-making process: trade-offs, gaming, and a future orientation. To this end, the applied urban anthropologist must master alien advice strategies like erecting priority hierarchies, making projections, and taking political stands as to the best of alternate futures. Further, the anthropologist's typically qualitative data will be largely indigestible to decision-makers and will thus have negligible policy impact unless translated into a usable form. In most cases this will require the anthropologist to report his data in some form of cost-benefit terminology. I am not suggesting here that we stop collecting qualitative data, only that we learn to quantify it. We must become sophisticated social accountants in order to communicate effectively with decision-makers.

The problems of communicating with community groups are quite different. The vehicle by which advice is transmitted is crucial here, as written research reports are often inefficient at best and patronizing at worst. Imagination is a necessity if the medium is not to interfere with the message (Alinsky 1971). For example, successful community organizers and consultants have found it necessary to disseminate data through lectures, slide shows, handouts, videotape, political demonstrations, and sophisticated graphics (Schensul 1973; Quinn 1974; Peattie 1970).

4. *We must streamline, augment, and rethink our traditional ethnographic methods.* While potentially valuable, the ethnographic method has been rarely applied to urban planning because, as traditionally designed, it is not easily operationalized in the urban environment. However, with three modifications, ethnographic fieldwork can be transformed into a useful planning tool. Like other urban planning data collection techniques, ethnography (particularly participation-observation) must be fitted to the time and action contingencies of political decision-making. Our standard twelve- or even six-month fieldwork project consumes far too much time and money. We must streamline. This will often involve sacrificing analytic rigor for immediate use

and impact. Without such a compromise, analytic meticulousness invariably turns to superfluous rigor as the urban decision-making process rushes past the applied ethnographer. I am not suggesting that we design sloppy research or that we generate inaccurate data; what I am calling for is a new, more realistic standard of quality for applied urban research.

The planning problems now facing our cities are too serious and pressing to permit the smug luxury of waiting for more perfect data. Margaret Mead, writing when anthropologists were applying their knowledge to the World War II effort, provides an appropriate mandate for today's applied urban anthropologist.

> There are those social scientists who are unwilling to use tools which they know to be clumsy when measured against what we may someday develop as a stone ax against an electric drill. They fear the fellow scientist who may review their work. Some of us feel that with every increase in knowledge . . . we should become stronger, not weaker, bolder, not more craven, freer to act. (Mead 1965:13)

The second modification requires us to rethink the assumed validity of our traditional unit of analysis. The traditional unit of analysis for ethnographers studying complex societies has been "the community," defined principally by co-residence. However, the urbanization process in this country has led to the decline of the co-residence group as a meaningful social unit. That is, compared to other variables, co-residence has relatively less explanatory power with respect to urban behavior. To understand urban behavior it is becoming more and more necessary to understand communities without propinquity (e.g., bureaucracies, citizen's committees, interest groups, drinking cliques, etc.), which are functionally bounded rather than territorally bounded. In light of this social transformation, applied urban anthropologists should be seriously questioning the usefulness of their traditional analytic unit. Yet, with the exception of scattered work in industrial anthropology (Pilcher 1972) and the network analysts (Whitten and Wolfe 1973) urban anthropologists continue to replicate the community studies as initially developed by Warner, Arensberg, Steward et al. Though these researchers continue to "discover" urban villages, we have clearly reached a point of diminishing returns.

Even where traditional communities exist in the city, rarely can the ethnographer's data be routinely accepted and used to generate planning policy. Urban neighborhoods are not primitive isolates; they are not even closely analogous to peasant communities. The complexity of the urban environment reshapes the significance of "streetcorner data." For example, unlike earlier community researchers we cannot assume the city's subunits to be microcosms of anything. Nor can we hope to understand community members' behavior without extensive data on the external political and economic constraints affecting them (Friedmann 1973b:ch.4).[6] This is not to say that community-level research has no place in applied urban anthropology. It does. But the anthropologist must recognize its limits as well as appreciate its advantages.

Assuming urban anthropologists eventually recognize the importance of communities without propinquity, they will be immediately confronted with a problem: How do we study them? My purpose in raising this issue is not to suggest specific solutions, although some have been offered (Bogdan 1972), but rather to point out the implications for training students for urban planning employment. That is, after convincing the student that applied urban anthropology is a worthy career and that he need not ship out to Pago Pago to be a "real" anthropologist, we cannot, in good conscience, continue to instruct him in ethnographic methods designed to describe and understand the Pago Pago. The few case studies reported demonstrate that simply applying traditional ethnographic methods to nontraditional communities will often result in failure (R. Nader 1975; L. Nader 1972; Foster and Kemper 1974).

The third modification involves augmenting the traditional natural history approach to ethnography—the ideal of observing behavior in its natural setting. If we are to make sense of these new nonresidential social units which now dominate urban society we must fortify the participant-observer's role and tool kit. One can only speculate as to the participant-observer's future forms and functions in urban planning. However, the potentials are infinite and I foresee rapid developments in this area with a proliferation of hyphenated participant roles on the street and in the literature (e.g., -interpreter, -analyst, -mediator, -innovator, -evaluator, -advocate, -organizer, ad infinitum).

A few anthropologists have already begun the necessary modifications and their work is worth mentioning here for the guidance it provides. The "small group culture" research of McFeat (1974) demonstrates that ethnographers can successfully study behavior in "non-natural" settings and exposes the artificial limitations imposed by the traditional natural history approach. Perhaps even more significant for the applied anthropologist is the related work of Agar (1973). Working with institutionalized addicts, he has demonstrated the validity and usefulness of behavioral data collected via observations in artificially replicated "natural" settings. These same techniques can be profitably utilized to conduct ethnographic studies within elusive, urban social units of great interest to urban planners (e.g., condominium owners' associations, ad hoc citizens' committees, etc.).

The above studies reveal the great potential of modifications such as experimental and artificial observation techniques and settings. If we are willing to move anthropology "indoors" we can make vital contributions to urban social planning with this augmented tool kit.

5. *We must identify and court new patrons and clients.* Our efforts here should be conducted largely in the federal arena. Our traditional federal patrons can be of little service as we confront the city. More appropriate patrons must be found. Fortunately, they exist in abundance. Since 1960, the federal government has created nearly a hundred programs to assist in meeting urban needs. However, with few exceptions, these programs are unfamiliar to anthropologists. We must master the intricacies of a new set of federal agencies with strange abbreviations like SSHR, SSA, LEAA, and OCD, for these agencies control the funding for programs most pertinent to urban problem solving. This new funding environment is further confounded by the fact that much of the federal money becomes available only at the local level where the federal funding delivery system has created a maze of municipal bodies that are likely to compose the bulk of our future clients. We must thus become sensitive to local needs and the local agencies mandated to serve those needs.

We must keep abreast of the continually evolving federal enabling legislation, for these acts virtually define the direction and content of urban planning. A thorough knowledge of their intent and potential is critical if we are to play a part. For example, the Community Services Act, the Comprehensive Employment and Training Act, the Housing and Community Development Act, and the National Environmental Policy Act (NEPA) all provide anthropologists with applied urban research opportunities.

Of all the federal enabling legislation enacted to date, NEPA holds the most potential for anthropologists as planners, for it creates the field of social impact assessment. Unfortunately, the Environmental Impact Studies (EIS) completed to date have taken a rather narrow view of the concept of impact. They have concentrated on the natural environment and ignored the sociocultural impact of development. NEPA's wording is vague, and so the legal necessity to include a social impact assessment as part of the EIS has yet to be clarified. The potentials of NEPA and social impact assessment are now being explored by all the social science disciplines (C. P. Wolf 1974). Anthropologists have unfortunately come late to this effort and the work completed so far has failed to face squarely the legal mandate of impact assessment by simply conducting salvage ethnography. The formation of an informal Group on Social Impact of Environmental Modification at the 1974 American Anthropological Association meeting is an important first step. It must be aggressively pursued.

The identification and utilization of existing legislation represents only one-half of our task in the federal arena. We must also begin to take an active role in the legislative process itself in order to protect and enhance the potentials for social science input in urban-related programs. This will mean mastering unfamiliar and time-consuming strategies like testifying in Congress, monitoring pending bills, and writing legislation for congressional sponsors. With the exception of archeologists, anthropologists have been uninterested in such activities, to their detriment (Moss 1975). The impressive lobbying success of the archeologists, which has virtually created a public archeology profession (through Public Law 93-291), is testimony to the potentials and necessity of this type of activity.

6. *We must seek new pathways to influence.* The pages of *Human Organization* are filled with debates over the proper role for the applied anthropologist. Through the 1960's, most anthropologists—concerned principally with means over ends—argued for some form of value-free, technocrat role. However, dismayed by Third World eruptions and disillusioned by the subsequent accusations of "their natives" (e.g., Batalla 1966), a significant minority of applied anthropologists during the 1970's began calling for their colleagues to take advocacy roles and responsibility for ends as well as means. These critics correctly perceived that our discipline's intellectual heritage of social Darwinism and democratic liberalism had ill-equipped us to confront the phenomenon of power. Eric Wolf is one of the more persuasive members of this critical wing and his solution to the dilemma is representative. He suggests that one way to mitigate our powerlessness is "to engage ourselves in a systematic writing of a history of the modern world in which we spell out the processes of power which created the present day cultural system and linkages between them" (E. Wolf 1969:10). Wolf's solution is curious for it represents no less a retreat from power than the stand taken by the despised technocrats. Simply "studying up" (L. Nader 1972) will not magically change the balance of power, for such a role only perpetuates the traditional separation of anthropological statuses from decision-making

statuses. If we ever are to implant anthropological perspectives and methods in the urban planning process, if our discipline is ever going to influence any policy to any significant degree, we must ourselves seek to achieve statuses of public decision-making.[7] With regard specifically to urban planning, the following statuses would provide public decision-making power: an elected planning commissioner, a civil servant position in a municipal planning department, or an appointment to a citizen's advisory board.

I should interject here that I am not dismissing the potential need for alternative power-seeking strategies outside our constituted institutions, nor am I advocating that all anthropologists aspire to public office. I recommend only that we recognize and legitimate the importance of public decision-making statuses and that we support our colleagues and train our students for their attainment. If we remain aloof from these power statuses, we doom ourselves to what Harvey (1973) has labeled "emotional tourism": visitors to the city passionately proclaiming its inadequacies while packing for home.

NOTES

I am grateful to Peter Snyder, John Friedmann, Lisa Peattie, and Irma Honigmann for reading and insightfully commenting on an earlier draft of this paper.

[1]For the past six years the author has worked as an applied urban anthropologist in a variety of roles: urban migration and housing design research, consultant to government agencies and community groups, and research associate in the UCLA School of Architecture and Urban Planning.

[2]I have purposely portrayed planning and anthropology as distinct—albeit complementary—activities in an effort to present clearly the argument for the necessity of an anthropological role in the urban planning process. The argument must be convincing, for it is my experience that anthropologists will not gain entry into the practice of urban planning unchallenged by the majority of planning professionals and by academic disciplines with a prior vested interest in the urban environment (e.g., political science, geography, social welfare, management, economics, and sociology). Initially at least, anthropology's expansion into the city will be most closely analogous to predatory adaptation rather than peaceful adaptive radiation into unoccupied environments. Unfortunately, this competition over urban turf is counterproductive to the planning effort. It is my hope that such adversary relationships will fade along with the archaic discipline and professional boundaries. Our urban problems will be more intelligently investigated when it becomes no longer necessary to ask whether an individual is a planner, an anthropologist, an economist, or a sociologist.

[3]For example, see the contents of Clifton's (1970) recent reader, which has gained popularity as a text in applied anthropology courses.

[4]This is not to imply that I am in total disagreement with the contributors to Hymes's volume (1974). Many of their criticisms have merit, but I believe they have overreacted and thus failed to identify the key locus for change in the discipline. To contribute to the urban planning process we need not reinvent anthropology; rather, we must reinvent the anthropologist. Successful

applied urban anthropologists must have a passion for problem-solving and a commitment to advocate social intervention. We must somehow reclaim these qualities for ourselves and instill them in our students.

[5]Eclecticism entails both benefits and costs. An important cost to consider is the eventual overload of requisite knowledge. This accumulated burden of information can be especially counterproductive in graduate training—particularly if the training is designed for nontraditional employment. Thus for programs of applied anthropology, judicial subtraction may become a corollary to eclectic addition. This will necessitate a painful assessment of traditional curricula.

[6]A small group of urban anthropologists have recently begun to confront this problem with what has become known as the "city-as-context" (see Rollwagen 1972 and the entire Spring 1975 issue of *Urban Anthropology*). However, anthropologists still have much to learn in this area—particularly from regional planners (for an excellent collection of this work see Friedmann and Alonso 1975).

[7]It is assumed, somewhat ideally, that once the anthropologist has achieved a decision-making status his role behavior will be guided by the anthropological perspective to the benefit of those touched by his policy decisions. The Jomo Kenyatta regime demonstrates that such a scenario is by no means inevitable.

REFERENCES

Agar, Michael, 1973. *Ripping and Running* (New York: Seminar Press).

Alinsky, Saul, 1971. *Rules for Radicals* (New York: Random House).

Argyris, Chris, 1974. *The Application of Organizational Sociology* (New York: Cambridge University Press).

Attneave, C. L., and R. V. Speck, 1974. Social Network Intervention in Time and Space. In *The Group as Agent of Change*, A. Jacobs and W. W. Spradlin, eds. (New York: Behavioral Publications), pp. 166-190.

Barnett, Homer C., 1956. *Anthropology in Administration* (Evanston, Ill: Row, Peterson).

Batalla, G. B., 1966. Conservative Thought in Applied Anthropology: A Critique. *Human Organization* 25:89-92.

Berry, B. J. L., ed., 1966. Comparative Factorial Ecology. *Economic Geography* (June Supplement).

Bogdan, Robert, 1972. *Participant Observation in Organizational Settings* (Syracuse, N.Y.: Syracuse University Press).

Bott, Elizabeth, 1957. *Family and Social Network* (New York: Free Press).

Bourne, Larry S., ed., 1971. *Internal Structure of the City: Readings on Space and Environment* (New York: Oxford University Press).

Braybrooke, Susan, 1974. Watching a People Watcher. *Design and Environment* 5:26-29.

Carlos, Manuel, and D. Brokensha, 1972. Agencies, Goals, and Clients: A Cross-Cultural Analysis. *Studies In Comparative International Development* 7:130-155.

Chapin, F. Stuart, 1974. *Human Activity Patterns in the City* (New York: Wiley Interscience).

Clifton, James A., ed., 1970. *Applied Anthropology: Readings in the Uses of the Science of Man* (Boston: Houghton Mifflin).

Davidson, R. T., 1974. *Chicano Prisoners* (New York: Holt, Rinehart and Winston).

Denfield, Duane, ed., 1974. *Streetwise Criminology* (Cambridge, Mass.: Schenkman).

Downs, James F., 1975. *Cultures in Crisis* (Beverly Hills: Glencoe Press).

Esber, George, 1972. Indian Housing for Indians. *Kiva* 37:141-147.
Everhart, Robert B., 1975. Problems of Doing Fieldwork in Educational Evaluation. *Human Organization* 34:204-215.
Faber, Mike, and Dudley Seers, 1972. *The Crisis in Planning* (London: Chatto and Windus).
Foster, George M., 1969. *Applied Anthropology* (Boston: Little, Brown).
Foster, G. M., and R. V. Kemper, eds., 1974. *Anthropologists in Cities* (Boston: Little, Brown).
Friedmann, John, 1973a. *Retracking America* (New York: Doubleday).
———, 1973b. *Urbanization, Planning and National Development* (Beverly Hills: Sage Publications).
Friedmann, John, and W. Alonzo, eds., 1975. *Regional Policy: Readings on Theory and Application* (Cambridge, Mass.: MIT Press).
Friedmann, John, and Barclay Hudson, 1974. Knowledge and Action: A Guide to Planning Theory. *Journal of the American Institute of Planners* 40:2-16.
Gans, Herbert J., 1962. *The Urban Villagers* (New York: Free Press).
———, 1971. Social Science for Social Policy. In *The Use and Abuse of Social Science*, I. L. Horowitz, ed. (New Brunswick, N. J.: Transaction Books), pp. 13-33.
Goodman, R., 1972. *After the Planners* (Baltimore: Penguin).
Grigsby, Gene E., and B. Campbell, 1974. A New Role for Planners: Working With Community Residents in Formulating Alternative Plans for Street Patterns Before Decision Making. *Transportation* 9:125-150.
Gulick, John, 1963. Urban Anthropology: Its Present and Future. *Transactions of the New York Academy of Sciences* (ser. 2) 25:445-458.
———, 1973. Urban Anthropology. In *Handbook of Social and Cultural Anthropology*, John Honigmann, ed. (Chicago: Rand McNally), pp. 979-1030.
Hall, Edward T., 1966. *The Hidden Dimension* (New York: Doubleday).
Hannerz, Ulf, 1969. *Soulside* (New York: Columbia University Press).
Hansen, N. M., ed.. 1972. *Growth Centers in Regional Economic Development* (New York: Free Press).
Harvey, David, 1973. *Social Justice and the City* (London: Edward Arnold).
Hymes, Dell, 1974. *Reinventing Anthropology* (New York: Random House).
Jacobs, James B., and H. G. Retsky, 1975. Prison Guard. *Urban Life* 4 (1):5-29.
Jacobs, Jerry, 1974. *Fun City* (New York: Holt, Rinehart and Winston).
Jacobs, Sue-Ellen, 1974. Doing It Our Way and Mostly for Our Own. *Human Organization* 33:380-382.
Johnson, N. J., and P. R. Sanday, 1971. Subcultural Variations in an Urban Poor Population. *American Anthropologist*, 73:128-143.
Jones, Richard P. 1974. Community Organization and Environmental Control, Phase II: Master Overview. (San Diego: San Diego County Office of Environmental Management).
Kaplan, David, and R. A. Manners, 1972. *Culture Theory* (Englewood Cliffs, N.J.: Prentice-Hall).
Kaplan, Marshall. 1974. *Urban Planning in the 1960s* (Cambridge, Mass.: MIT Press).
Kelling, G. L., et al., 1974. *The Kansas City Preventive Patrol Experiment, A Summary Report* (Washington, D.C.: Police Foundation).
Kessler, Evelyn S., 1974. *Anthropology: The Humanizing Process* (New York: Allyn and Bacon).
Leichter, H. J., and W. E. Mitchell, 1967. *Kinship and Casework* (New York: Russell Sage Foundation).
Lewis, Oscar, 1966. The Culture of Poverty. *Scientific American* 215:19-25.
Liebow, Elliot, 1967. *Tally's Corner* (Boston: Little, Brown).

Llewelyn-Davies, Richard 1975. The Role of the Social Sciences in Architecture and Planning. In *Anthropology and Society*, B. Maday, ed. (Washington D.C.: Anthropological Society of Washington), pp. 46-53.

Lurie, Nancy O., 1955. Anthropology and Indian Claims Litigation: Problems, Opportunities and Recommendations. *Ethnohistory* 2:357-375.

McFeat, Tom, 1974. *Small Group Cultures* (New York: Pergamon Press).

Marx, Karl 1927. Misère de la philosophie. In *Marx-Engels Gesamtausgabe*, Volume I., D. Rigzanov, ed. (Moscow: Marx-Engels Institute). (First published in 1847.)

Matthiasson, Carolyn J., 1974. Coping in a New Environment: Mexican Americans in Milwaukee, Wisconsin. *Urban Anthropology* 3:262-277.

Mead, Margaret, 1956. Applied Athropology, 1955. In *Some Uses of Anthropology: Theoretical and Applied*, J. B. Casagrande and T. Gladwin, eds. (Washington, D.C.: Anthropological Society of Washington), pp. 94-108.

————, 1965, *And Keep Your Powder Dry* (2nd ed.; New York: William Morrow). (First published in 1942.)

Moss, Frank E., 1975. Anthropology in Legislation. In *Anthropology and Society*, B. Maday, ed. (Washington, D.C.: Anthropological Society of Washington), pp. 76-83.

Mydral, Gunner, 1958. *Value in Social Theory* (New York: Harper).

Nader, Laura, 1972. Up the Anthropologist—Perspectives Gained from Studying Up. In *Reinventing Anthropology*, Dell Hymes, ed. (New York: Random House), pp. 284-311.

Nader, Ralph, 1975. Anthropology in Law and Civic Action. In *Anthropology and Society*, B. Maday, ed. (Washington, D.C.: Anthropological Society of Washington), pp. 31-40.

Needleman, M. L., and C. E. Needleman, 1974. *Guerrillas in the Bureaucracy* (New York: Wiley).

Newman, Oscar, 1972. *Defensible Space* (New York: Macmillan).

Ogbu, John U., 1974. *The Next Generation* (New York: Academic Press).

Padfield, Harland, and Ray Williams, 1973. *Stay Where You Were* (New York: Lippincott).

Partridge, W. L., 1973. *The Hippie Ghetto* (New York: Holt, Rinehart and Winston).

Paul, Benjamin D., 1955. *Health, Culture and Community* (New York: Russell Sage Foundation).

Peattie, Lisa, 1968. Reflections on Advocacy Planning. *Journal of the American Institute of Planners* 34:80-87.

————, 1970. Drama and Advocacy Planning. *Journal of the American Institute of Planners* 36:405-410.

————, 1975. Fieldwork and Planning (mimeograph; Cambridge, Mass.: MIT Department of Urban Studies and Planning).

Pilcher, William W., 1972. *The Portland Longshoremen* (New York: Holt, Rinehart and Winston).

Plotnicov, Leonard, 1974. Some Thoughts on Anthropological Research in Cities of Modern Society. *Comparative Urban Research* 4:5-22.

Quinn, Tom, 1974. NR: The Politics of Inner-City Communication. *Print* 28:60-67.

Rainwater, Lee, 1966. Fear and the House-As-Haven in the Lower Class. *Journal of the American Institute of Planners* 32:23-37.

————, 1970 *Behind Ghetto Walls* (Chicago: Aldine).

Rapoport, Amos, 1971. Some Observations Regarding Man-Environment Studies. *Architectural Research and Teaching* 2:4-15.

————, 1973. The Ecology of Housing. *Ekistics* 213:145-151.

Rollwagen, Jack R., 1972. A Comparative Framework for the Investigation of the City-as-context: A Discussion of the Mexican Case. *Urban Anthropology* 1:68-86.

Rosenfeld, Gerry, 1971. *Shut Those Thick Lips* (New York: Holt, Rinehart and Winston).

Rubinstein, Jonathan, 1973. *City Police* (New York: Ballantine).

Schensul, Stephen L., 1973. Action Research: The Applied Anthropologist in a Community Mental Health Program. In *Anthropology Beyond the University*, Alden Redfield, ed., Southern Anthropological Society Proceedings, No. 7 (Athens: University of Georgia Press), pp. 106-119.

Selznick, Philip, 1949. *TVA and the Grass Roots* (Los Angeles: University of California Press).

Shiloh, Ailon, 1966. *The Total Institution: Profiles of Mental Patient Perception and Adaptation* (Downey, Ill.: U.S. Veterans Administration).

Snyder, Peter Z., 1973. Social Interaction Patterns and Relative Urban Success: The Denver Navajo. *Urban Anthropology* 2:1-24.

Sommer, Robert, 1969. *Personal Space* (Englewood Cliffs, N.J.: Prentice-Hall).

Spicer, Edward H., 1952. *Human Problems in Technological Change* (New York: Russell Sage Foundation).

Spicer, E. H., and T. E. Downing, 1974. Training for Non-Academic Employment: Major Issues. In *Training Programs for New Opportunities in Applied Anthropology*, E. Leacock, N. L. Gonzalez, and G. Kushner, eds. (Washington, D.C.: American Anthropological Association), pp. 1-12.

Spradley, James P., 1973. The Ethnography of Crime in American Society. In *Cultural Illness and Health*, L. Nader and T. W. Maretzki, eds. (Washington, D.C.: American Anthropological Society), pp. 23-34.

Stack, Carol B., 1974. *All our Kin* (New York: Harper and Row).

Stanton, Esther, 1970. *Clients Come Last* (Beverly Hills: Sage Publications).

Suttles, Gerald, 1972. *The Social Construction of Communities* (Chicago: University of Chicago Press).

Tax, Sol, 1958. The Fox Project. *Human Organization* 17:17-19.

Theodorson, George A., 1961. *Studies in Human Ecology* (Evanston, Ill.: Row, Peterson).

Valentine, Charles, 1966. *Culture and Poverty: Critique and Counter Proposals* (Chicago: University of Chicago Press).

————, 1974. *Black Studies and Anthropology: Scholarly and Political Interests in Afro-American Culture* (Reading, Mass.: Addison-Wesley Modular Publications).

Waddell, J. O., and O. M. Watson, 1971. *The American Indian in Urban Society* (Boston: Little, Brown).

Weaver, Thomas, ed., 1973. *To See Ourselves* (Glenview, Ill.: Scott, Foresman).

Wellman, David, 1968. The Wrong Way to Find Jobs for Negroes. *Trans-Action* 5(5):9-18.

Weppner, R. S., 1973. An Anthropological View of the Street Addict's World. *Human Organization* 32:111-122.

Whitten, N. E., and A. W. Wolfe, 1973. Network Analysis. In *Handbook of Social and Cultural Anthropology*, John Honigmann, ed. (Chicago: Rand McNally), pp. 717-746.

Wilson, James Q., 1968. *City Politics and Public Policy* (New York: Wiley).

Wolcott, H. F., 1973. *The Man in the Principal's Office* (New York: Holt, Rinehart and Winston).

Wolf, C. P., ed., 1974. *Social Impact Assessment* (Milwaukee: Environmental Design Research Association).

Wolf, Eric, 1969. American Anthropologists and American Society. In *Concepts* and *Assumptions in Contemporary Anthropology*, Stephen Tyler, ed., Southern Anthropological Society Proceedings, No. 3 (Athens: University of Georgia Press), pp. 3-11.

Wulff, Robert M. 1973. *Housing the Papago: An Analytical Critique of a Housing Delivery System.* International Housing Productivity Study Research Report (Los Angeles: UCLA School of Architecture and Urban Planning).

Yin, Robert K., 1972. *Participant-Observation and the Development of Urban Neighborhood Policy* (New York: New York Rand Institute).

Zimmerman, Don H., 1974. Fact as a Practical Accomplishment. In *Enthnomethodology*, R. Turner, ed. (Baltimore: Penguin), pp. 128-143.

Cognitive Anthropology and Applied Problems in Education

ATTEMPTS to grapple with political, ethical, and professional dilemmas confronting anthropology are reflected in the partitionings of the sub-field of applied anthropology. Familiar demarcations include "action anthropology," "advocacy anthropology," and now, the "new applied anthropology." Although many of the political and ethical issues associated with applied anthropology are of particular concern to me, they are bypassed in this paper. Also omitted is any consideration of vexing logistical problems, such as maintaining professional status or communicating effectively with clients, which typically confront the applied anthropologist. These areas have been neglected in order to focus upon the question of the practical relevance of anthropological expertise. The discussion here concerns the utility of a particular set of anthropological methods and concepts for action-generating research addressed to contemporary social problems.

In response to a request to name his specialty, a colleague of mine once surprised an inquirer by answering, "applied ethnographic semantics." Especially for those who associate the term "cognitive anthropology" with the study of domains such as firewood, the notion that methods and concepts from cognitive anthropology are useful in examining contemporary social problems might appear incredible. In actuality, systematic knowledge of belief systems is pertinent to a number of applied problem areas, including education.

The subfield of anthropology and education has evolved largely in response to contemporary problems. Education, in contrast to other institutions (e.g., religious institutions), is seen as an appropriate target for intervention by academics—including anthropologists. Much to the distress of those who favor maintaining a dispassionate posture, a number of anthropologists have been quite vocal in their concern about current educational problems (Wolcott 1971). Recent theoretical formulations as well indicate an awareness of contemporary educational issues (Gearing and Tindall 1973; Gearing et al. n.d.; Gearing 1973; Spindler 1974). The preliminary work in the area, the concern with contemporary problems, and the type of theoretical formulation occurring in the subfield of anthropology and education provide a congenial context for specialized methods such as those utilized by cognitive anthropologists.

The projects to be described in this paper include identification of a problem hampering the use of a particular educational resource; a preplanning study designed to minimize problems with the use of a future educational facility; and the development of a position paper and a research plan pertaining to poor school performance by ethnic minority children. To indicate how cognitive or emic methods can be useful for any of these diverse problems, the underlying themes and research strategies associated with cognitive anthropology are presented briefly in the next section of the paper. The third section describes the three problems mentioned above. In the final section, I will argue that for certain applied problems there are sound reasons for studying emic systems in the detail prescribed by cognitive methods.

An important assumption underlying cognitive anthropology asserts that language is a key element in understanding and anticipating culturally patterned behavior. Cognitive anthropology exploits the relationship between language and cognitive systems in order to explain behavior. It is postulated that knowledge of the world as the actor sees it is a more direct guide to behavior than knowledge of the characteristics of that to which the actor responds. From this perspective, it becomes important to determine the actor's view, the categories he uses, and the beliefs he associates with these categories. It is further assumed that a significant portion of these categories and beliefs are easily expressed in the actor's language and therefore elicitable from him.[1]

Initially, writers such as Conklin (1964), Frake (1964b), and Goodenough (1965) suggested standards of descriptive adequacy for ethnography which are reminiscent of criteria for evaluating grammars in linguistics. To be adequate, a grammar must be able to generate and assess sentences according to grammaticality, distinguishing grammatical sentences from ungrammatical ones. Analogously, a descriptively adequate ethnography must be sufficient to generate and assess behavioral strings according to cultural appropriateness. (See also Burling 1969; Williams 1973.)

Many of the initial research efforts in the cognitive field centered upon descriptive semantics. The problem of specifying referential meaning was attacked using a variety of methods, including componential analysis and formal semantic analysis as developed by Lounsbury (1964a,b). In addition, techniques and quasi-experimental tasks such as triads, semantic differential, belief matrices, and judged similarity were employed to test the "psychological reality" of competing analyses. (See, for example, Goodenough 1956, 1964, 1965; Romney and D'Andrade 1964; Wallace and Atkins 1960; Burton 1972; D'Andrade et al. 1972; Szalay and D'Andrade 1972; Pollnac 1975.)

In addition to descriptive semantics or ethnosemantics, there also developed an emphasis on the study of multilexeme constructions interlinking items from disparate semantic domains. These constructions are formed by combining a question frame (e.g., "children learn ―― in school?") with an elicited response (e.g., "to read") to produce a statement such as "children learn to read in school." Metzger (1973) refers to these constructions as "assertions," considering them to represent beliefs held about the constituent categories of the domains. Belief systems from this vantage point are construed as sets of beliefs at varying levels of specificity depending on the inclusiveness of the constituent components. The beliefs are not equivalent to, but rather are represented by, elicitable assertions.[2]

Along a related line, anthropologists also became interested in the speaker's ability to assess the truth value of statements. Although the generative or transformational grammarians have taken the speaker's ability to judge the grammaticality of what to him are novel utterances as a criterion which a grammar must meet to satisfy standards of adequacy, they have generally concerned themselves with syntactic compliance only—even though speakers, according to some reports, exhibit greater consensus on judgments about agreement (i.e., truth) than they do on judgments about grammaticality (Stefflre et al. 1971). The set of rules and principles which are functionally equivalent to the speaker's competence in judging the truth value of statements has been referred to by Stefflre et al. as a "grammar of agreement." Such a grammar or belief system enables an individual to judge the truth value of syntactically possible native language statements such as "children learn to read in school" or "chiropracters effectively treat cancer." The nature of the rules of a grammar of agreement has received only limited attention. The process by which people are able to judge the truth value of statements is unknown, although it is probably true that they do not have stored in their memories lists of combinations of items and attributes with the appropriate indication as to whether the resulting assertions are true or not (D'Andrade et al. 1972).[3]

An important aspect of the proposed relationship between language and behavior is the basis it provides for predicting behavior toward both familiar and novel items. People daily encounter objects, ideas, people, and programs which they classify as examples of a familiar category. Somewhat less regularly perhaps, they encounter a novel item that varies sufficiently from the items to which it is similar so that a distinction is made, and it is recognized as a heretofore unclassified incidence of some superordinate taxon. In classifying the novel item, the set of common expectations associated with other members of the contrast set become associated with the novel item. A new instance of an old category is related to as though it were equivalent to other members of the category, while an instance of a new category is related to as a member of a familiar superordinate taxon having some special difference that distinguishes it from other members of the taxon.[4] If there is knowledge about how an item (any item, including a novel one) is described by an actor, then the behavioral response to that item can be anticipated. Correspondence between "rules" derived from category-assertion systems and behavior has been demonstrated in a number of cases.[5]

Description of new services, objects, or programs may be prepared by program designers who are unaware of the perspectives of the potential users of the service. Problems frequently arise when clients are attracted to the program by descriptions that they later come to feel were inaccurate. Additionally, if the source of the problem is not apparent, both providers and clients may be at a loss to explain the frustrations that each encounters when expectations are not met.

As mentioned in the previous section, methods for ascertaining actor category-assertion systems have been devised. Some of these methods were used in a study commissioned by a preschool chain, the Richardson (a pseudonym) preschools, run by professional educators who take pride in the educational methods used in their programs. They commissioned the study because their schools were being subscribed to at a rate that fell below their expectations. They wished to know the reasons for the low enrollment rate.

The study was designed to investigate parents' perceptions of preschools. We first obtained parent categories of preschools and beliefs about each type of preschool. Next, using a fairly large sample (N=300), we asked people to rank descriptions and names of types of preschools according to preference. For this ranking we included descriptions of the Richardson preschools taken directly from Richardson advertisements. We also included descriptions created by parents whose children were enrolled in a Richardson preschool.

The parent descriptions of the Richardson preschools were quite different from the chain's advertisements. We found that the type described in the Richardson advertisements was seen as very similar to a type of day care center referred to in the trade as "Mom and Pop" day care centers. The Richardson descriptions of the preschools indicated to parents that the preschools were day care oriented and run by nonprofessionals. Parents with children enrolled in a Richardson preschool, on the other hand, produced descriptions of the schools which the large sample responded to as similar to the Montessori variety of preschools. When parents interested in the type of day care center described in the advertisements visited the preschool to find out the particulars, they discovered a preschool that differed considerably from the Mom and Pop type. This discrepancy was especially apparent with regard to price. Thus, the preschool chain, through its own self-description which did not correspond to how people actually perceived it, was attracting a number of parents who were not really interested in what it offered and hence not inclined to enroll their children.

Additional problems of a perceptual nature may arise when new programs are introduced. These problems are not restricted to services offered by commercial firms; they arise just as easily in cases where new programs are introduced by a government or even a community-based local organization.[6]

In the Richardson example given above, the disparity between what parents expected and what they encountered when they arrived was fairly evident. The situation might have been more complicated. If the price had been lower, parents unconcerned about the educational aspects might have considered the preschool acceptable as a day care center and behaved as though it were a day care center. In other words, they could have simply perceived a use for the school that the Richardson educators had not anticipated. Had the differences in perspective remained unrecognized, the educators might constantly have felt that they were fighting their clients in order to deliver the service they felt they had agreed to provide. Glazer (1963) describes a case of perceptions of public schools which may very well have caused such problems. South Italian immigrants to the United States in the late nineteenth and early twentieth centuries tended not to see a role for education in America although they had a strong desire for material improvement. They believed that one's circumstances improved with hard work and luck, not by wasting time in schools that were taught by women who did not even beat the children.

It is hardly a new discovery that service users' perspectives may differ from those of service providers. It is also commonplace that service users whose perspectives differ from those of service planners may utilize an item in a manner not envisioned by the planners or imagined by providers. The disparity between perspectives, of course, is often pronounced when services are imported or imposed across cultural lines.

In the Richardson preschool example, the service providers, although set apart by their professional perspective, did have the same general cultural background as their clients. In the situation discussed in this section, the service providers, who were Anglo architects, differed in cultural background as well as in professional perspective from their clients, who were Navajo. The architects in this example were aware that their clients might have different beliefs and expectations from their own and thus made a special effort to obtain community input.

The Ramah Navajo High School is a community-controlled school begun by a community corporation during the Nixon administration. Following the school's inception, the school board petitioned and received funds from Congress to construct a new facility for the school. Initially the school was housed in an old building located in the predominantly Mormon town of Ramah, New Mexico. The Navajo community desired more appropriate facilities and a more appropriate location. To develop the new facilities, the school board hired a Berkeley-based architectural firm with a reputation for social awareness.

The architects felt they had insufficient knowledge about the community's desires for the center and the cultural patterns which might affect the kind of space that would be necessary. They sought to design a structure that would be consistent with the community members' expectations about architectural style and anticipated that, due to cultural differences, Navajo feelings about architecture might not coincide with those of Anglos. They rejected the alternative often adopted in such situations of designing structures to fit "traditional native architecture." They were not content simply to select what to them were significant aspects of Navajo style. Instead, they felt that a study to determine what the people believed to be appropriate was a necessary part of their design process. With the approval of the Ramah Navajo school board, we accepted from the architectural firm the job of gathering information pertinent to the design of the new school and community center building (Harding, Clement, and Lammers 1973).

The data were obtained using a combination of techniques for elicting perceptions of and preferences for building types and architectural styles. The data indicated that while certain aspects of traditional architecture were desired for the new center, others were not. Certain aspects of the hogan shape were desired; the traditional materials were not. Traditional hogans, for example, have rough interiors. For their school and community center, the Navajos wanted soft, smooth textures and surfaces plus the latest in equipment. Preferences for windows were fairly complex. In general, the people sampled wished to have windows in the building (as opposed to the hogan style of no windows), but they did not like the interior of the building to be visible from the outside. They wanted to be able to see out, to enjoy what could be seen outside, but they did not wish to be viewed by persons outside the building. The vertical size of a building was also important. Many of the respondents had a vague sense that multi-story buildings are dangerous, although impressive. There was also a strong dislike of buildings that appear to be unoccupied.

In addition to information on architectural types and features, we attempted to determine what events the Navajo thought might take place at the school and community center and the activities they associated with such events. They mentioned numerous specific activities associated with learning standard academic skills. Concern was expressed that provision be made for some type of health care at the center. Associated activities included dental care, x-ray services, handling emergencies, and housing the sick. Athletic events were considered important, as were vocational courses, adult education, and learning traditional Navajo skills such as tanning, dyeing, leatherworking, silversmithing, and weaving.

Eliciting events and activities associated with curriculum preferences was important since the school board and administrators have considerable autonomy in determining curriculum and teaching style. These elicitations also proved important in determining what was and was not perceived as appropriate in the school and community center context. For example, plans for the school originally drawn up by the Bureau of Indian Affairs (BIA) included a dining room, a living room, and a kitchen, to be used in teaching homemaking. The Navajos, in contrast to the BIA designers, anticipated instruction in Navajo home-making skills — a desire requiring different types of equipment and facilities.

The results of the study appear to have been useful in assisting the architects to approximate a design that the Navajo would see as appropriate for their center. The architects' first design, developed in light of the findings of the study, was enthusiastically received by the board members and others in attendance at the chapter meeting at which it was presented. In contrast to the usual process, the designs did not have to be redone two or three times after successive reviews by the client. No follow-up study has been undertaken to ascertain to what extent the buildings themselves are seen to incorporate positive versus negative features. Additional evaluation of this type would pro-vide a critical test of the usefulness of the study to the preplanning process.

The examples considered above refer to the identification or anticipa-tion of problems arising from clients' reactions to educational services and facilities. To complete the paradigm, it might be supposed that clients are affected by the way service personnel in institutions react to them. Some individuals seeking services find that they are considered inappropriate as clients by functionaries providing the services. This phenomenon has been hypothesized as a link in the chain of factors affecting the educational attainment of black, Puerto Rican, American Indian, and other ethnic minority children in the United States.

Anthropologists, in addition to others in contact with educational institutions serving ethnic minorities, have argued that school func-tionaries, policy-makers, and developers of educational materials hold unwarranted conceptualizations about the cultures of ethnic minority students. There is no doubt that assumptions made about ethnic minor-ity children are not always positive. The adaptation of ethnic minority children to the generally hostile or negative atmospheres they confront in school has been commented upon in a number of studies (Rosenfeld 1971; Fuchs 1969; Leacock 1969; Rist 1970, 1972; Wax and Wax 1971; Valentine 1971).[7]

Interestingly, Frederick Gearing and his associates in developing a general cultural theory of education have singled out interactional parameters as being of primary importance in the transmission of knowledge. Gearing and his associates (Gearing and Tindall 1973; Gearing et al. n.d.; Gearing 1973) have postulated that the differential distribution of knowledge in a society cannot be explained by problems of getting knowledge into people's heads; rather, the spread of knowledge is prevented for the most part by barriers that systematically arise between certain types of individuals. These barriers arise and are mediated in accordance with the learned cognitive mappings upon which individuals base their expectations of proper behavior for those with whom they interact.[8]

Recently, I had the opportunity to work with a multidisciplinary team funded by the National Institute of Education to formulate a position paper (J. A. Johnson 1973) and a research proposal on minority education. This team focused upon the teacher-student relationship as it affects low-income black children during their early years. Consistent with the increasing awareness of the social context of learning, we were interested in factors that affect the child's interactions with school personnel, who distribute reinforcement, knowledge, and certification. The argument that formed the basis of the research hypotheses bears some resemblance to that associated with Rosenthal's research, the gist of which has come to be known popularly as the self-fulfilling prophecy. (See, for example, Rosenthal and Jacobson 1968.) Rosenthal's research, and the attempted replications (numbering in the hundreds) of his studies, however, have been focused primarily on only one source of information, test scores, used by teachers to form expectations of children. The research team decided to consider other sources of information, including behavioral patterns. In particular, we considered how teachers might be using behavioral patterns that are culturally appropriate in the child's home community, but not in the eyes of the school personnel, as a source of information for classifying students according to their potential success in school. We were concerned with the complex interactive effect of the teacher's implicit categorization of the student. Our research design included steps for investigating teachers' categories of children using methods from cognitive anthropology.[9] We were interested in how children are categorized, the referential meanings of the categories, the beliefs associated with the categories, and the behavioral differences of teachers toward various children which can be explained by these categorizations and beliefs.

The research hypotheses sketched above suggest a fairly complex set of variables affecting school performance. In addition, of course, there are many other ideas about factors producing variance in educational attainment.[10] The persistence of the problem despite the plethora of hypotheses advanced as possible explanations for the variation indicates that research modes that simply produce and explore hypotheses may no longer be useful. To investigate complicated processes and to uncover the numerous behavioral links hypothesized, complex research designs are necessary. It is also clear from the position paper and research design generated by the multidisciplinary team with which I worked that the problem is a complex one for which many different disciplines have something valuable to contribute, both in terms of conceptualization and research methods.

The work of other anthropologists interested in education indicates their awareness of many competing hypotheses concerning educational phenomena and of the need for cooperation between disciplines. Some have emphasized the development of culturally valid instruments and explicit research procedures that can be tested for reliability (Spindler 1973, 1974; Burnett 1973). Potentially, methods such as those mentioned in this paper, and others developing along similar lines, can be used to test hypotheses developed from anthropological orientations toward sociocultural phenomena. Heretofore, perspectives characteristic of anthropology have been noticeably absent from many of the approaches adopted to handle contemporary social problems.

The strategies used in the three studies I have described may be considered in more general terms. Particularly, they may be viewed in terms of the levels of specificity of cultural description necessary for practical problems.

Stefflre (n.d.) has described a device encompassing objectives for description of nonverbal behavior that are roughly similar to those objectives a grammar must meet for linguistic behavior. Stefflre refers to this device as a "behavioral dictionary." The dictionary would contain the following information:

1. An enumeration of the basic linguistic forms in the language—including for each lexeme an indication of the contrast classes (superordinate taxa) to which it belongs, a referential rule of use, and beliefs about and behavior toward instances of this category not predictable from its contrast classes.

2. A description of the word class structures found in the language—including for each contrast class the elements of its contrast set, the rule for inclusion of new elements, beliefs about and behavior toward all members of the contrast set plus exceptions.

3. Combinatorial rules for short simple utterances—including (a) statements as to which classes can combine to form grammatical, sensible, and true utterances and (b) statements as to the manner in which the meanings of the classes interact referentially, in terms of beliefs and in terms of behavior.

Theoretically, such a dictionary would enable one to predict the response to any object, event, idea, role, or program introduced into the culture. Predictions could be made as to how the item would be described as well as the beliefs and behaviors associated with it. Each set of data described in the previous sections could be viewed as comprising a portion of such a behavioral dictionary, albeit an infinitesimal part with very limited predictive use outside the domain of study.

Obviously, the scope of the task outlined by Stefflre is massive. (In 1965, he estimated the cost of building such a dictionary to be more than a quarter of a million dollars.) The size of the task suggests the scope of the endeavor implicit in the goals set by the new ethnographers.

A common criticism of ethnoscience is that it is the science of trivia (see Harris 1968, for example). The new ethnography, in other words, has been criticized as demanding emic detail beyond what is useful or necessary for ethnography. One approach to this issue of excessive detail is to view it as a problem of specificity of cultural rules or, perhaps more appropriately, beliefs. If a hundred specific beliefs and the associated behaviors clarified by them can be derived from one general rule, then it is more economical to concentrate on the general rule than on the specific beliefs.

For practical problems of the type described above, however, it seems clear that at least in terms of our present limited ability to link general characteristics or rules with specific behavior, we must not assume applicability of general rules in all contexts where logically they might be expected to apply. A comment by Firth concerning the practical utility of ethnographic research illustrates the problem to which I am referring:

> It is often said nowadays that a medical man should learn "something" about the customs and beliefs of the people among whom he is going to work. But *what* precisely does he need to learn? An unsystematic collection of scraps of information may lead to an exaggerated respect for taboos and an under-estimation of the importance of features of the society which may throw a medical program out of gear. (1959:153)

Firth's comment implies that we simply do not know which of the cultural patterns distilled in ethnographic research will be operative in any given situation. Recalling the Ramah Navajo High School, many of the responses or feelings about architectural styles collected in our study could be explained after the fact or retrodicted from studies of Navajo culture. The practice of abandoning hogans in which someone has died and the negative associations with deserted hogans reported by Kluckhohn and Leighton (1962), for example, could easily be related to our respondents' concern with whether buildings look deserted. It is also possible, however, that any number of sets of findings including those which actually did occur could have similarly been retrodicted. In other words, it seems that it would have been very difficult to know beforehand exactly what aspects of the traditional styles and beliefs would be relevant in this situation.

There has been little attention devoted to the problem of specifying conditions under which a given cultural pattern will be manifest. Rather there seems to be a general assumption that beliefs are consistent across levels of specificity. Studies in which different levels are explicitly compared, however, tend to show that more generalized beliefs may not be consistent with choices made on more specific levels. To cite an example from anthropology and education research, Spindler (1974), in a study of beliefs about village life versus city life in a small town in southern Germany, found that for the school children the symbolic value of the village differs from the symbolic value of the city. The majority of children, as well as the parents and teachers interviewed, preferred the village to the city. The village was favored because of fresh air, less traffic, quietness, nearness to nature, and friendliness. The city was seen as being noisy, dangerous, without space to play and walk, impersonal, and as having bad air. According to Spindler's research, the general preference of village over city life is consistent with the symbolic qualities associated with the village versus the city that are transmitted through certain activities in school. Spindler also investigated preferences for what he calls instrumental (goal-related)activities. The version of the Instrumental Activities Inventory (IAI) devised by Spindler paired instrumental activities available in the village with contrasting activities available in the city. When the children were asked to choose between village instrumentality versus city instrumentality they tended to choose he latter. The majority opted for modern apartment houses, white collar office jobs, and work as a machinist or as a technical draftsman rather than alternatives which were clearly village- and land-oriented. The reasons given were pragmatic, such as better pay, more security, and cleaner working conditions. In summarizing the results of the study,

Spindler describes the apparent role of the children's idealized value orientation toward the village:

> What is the cognitive depth of this identity? The responses to the I.A.I. pictures seem only partly governed by this identity. Pragmatic considerations seem to become important when respondents are faced with finite instrumental choices. The village-land-nature identity, then, may be regarded as idealized, perhaps even as "spurious" in that it cannot be applied consistently in the real choices presented in an urbanizing environment. Nevertheless, this idealized identity could be important as a cohesive force binding together apparently divergent elements of the total population. (1974:266)

The relationship between beliefs that refer to fairly global concepts and more specific beliefs (which Spindler calls instrumental activities) has been shown to be dubious in other studies as well. Nickerson and Hochstrasser (1970), for example, in examining reasons given by refusers of a tuberculin skin test in eastern Kentucky, noted that refusers (who formed only a small percentage of those to whom the test was offered) rarely proffered a reason for the refusal which bore any connection to the fatalistic beliefs that are supposedly an important cultural characteristic of the southern Appalachian folk culture as revealed in fundamentalist religious beliefs. It is also interesting to note that Stekert's (1970) explanation of southern Appalachian migrants' relatively low use of modern medical facilities available to them in Detroit as an expression of fatalism has been criticized by Pearsal and Abrahams. (See Pearsal's and Abraham's comments appended to the Stekert article.) They criticize such generalizations about cultural emphases of southern Appalachian whites on the basis that these general characteristics are not in evidence in all contexts and thus cannot be simply retrodictively invoked without regard for other possible factors.[11]

Indications that the relationship between general and specific cultural "rules" are at best very loose are also in line with recent theoretical formulations. Rappaport (1971a,b, 1974), for example, argues that more general rules tend to refer to concepts that are abstract, vague, and ambiguous. The importance of these general rules, according to Rappaport, is that they serve the important function of validating the organizational system. They play a role in the epistemological system of a population in that, by being associated with these general rules or beliefs, the decisions emanating from the regulating mechanisms are sanctified and therefore adhered to so that the system may operate smoothly. People who believe that God's will prevails or that capitalism is the best economic system possible, for example, are not constrained to carry out the full implications that might logically be derived. Rather, the belief in God or capitalism is invoked to garner loyalty and compliance to what in effect may be arbitrary systems of the higher-order organization. Rappaport argues further that lower-level systems that are more closely articulated with extra-cultural factors are not necessarily logically derived from these more abstract rules but rather are more responsive to actual conditions. He suggests that the details of agricultural systems used in Russia and the United States, for example, are probably very similar even though the larger regulatory systems which subsume agriculture are supported by fairly disparate economic theories.

According to Rappaport, there is a sound reason for lack of correspondence between the more abstract and the more specific levels. Without the constraint that higher- and lower-order beliefs must be strongly interrelated, adaptation to changing conditions can come about on the more specific levels quite easily without necessitating a change in the entire belief system. Thus, a population may make a great number of adjustments yet maintain their higher-order cultural rules. Ambiguity with respect to the more general level rules allows for many alternatives and thus greater flexibility.

The implications of these arguments are that the study of specific beliefs is not simply a misguided love of detail in situations where an understanding of probable reaction to a particular type of event, object, idea, program, or person is required. Often there is a definite relationship between general beliefs and behavioral tendencies in particular contexts; however, the relationship need not be one-to-one in every case and must be tested when prediction or even accurate retrodiction is desired.

The fine detail of the data obtained through cognitive anthropological methods is useful and perhaps necessary for certain types of practical problems. Furthermore, the conceptual framework and the research skills involved in obtaining emic data, which is important for understanding the functioning of services, is one area in which applied anthropologists may make a unique contribution to the solution of contemporary problems.

NOTES

[1]Not all cognitive categories have monolexemic labels. Data supporting the existence of shared covert or nonlabeled categories are presented in Berlin, Breedlove, and Raven (1968).

[2]Goodenough (1963:147; 1971) and Tyler (1969:16) use the term *proposition* in place of Metzger's term *assertion*. A term in addition to *belief* is needed, to distinguish between a belief as a mentalistic construct and as a statement that reflects the belief. (See also Frake 1964a.)

[3]The D'Andrade et al. (1972) discussion concerns the ability of respondents to judge the truth value of the hundreds of questions posed in a beliefs matrix. A beliefs matrix, or an item-by-attributes matrix, is an interview format in which the respondent is asked to judge the truth value of statements formed by the combination of all the row items and all the column items. The items are generally derived from previous interviews. The purpose of the matrix is to determine the truth value of each item-attribute combination. It is also a device for securing a measure of distributional similarity for each pair of items. For further detail see Stefflre et al. 1971; D'Andrade et al. 1972; Harding 1973; and Clement 1974.

[4]For further detail see Goodenough 1963, 1971; Stefflre n.d. See Harding, Lammers et al. 1973 and Harding and Clement 1974 for an example of anticipation of response to novel items.

[5]Preference for descriptions of items has been found to be highly correlated with preference for the items themselves (Stefflre n.d.). Emic rules for residence choice have been found to account for actual residence practice in a study by Geoghegan (1969) in the southern Philippines. Emic rules for choice of crops for a given soil have been found to account for actual soil-crop combinations by Allen Johnson (1974) in a study he did in Brazil. My own data from American Samoa indicate that assertions connecting health resources with health problems are reflected in behavior. The health problems associated with the hospitals and dispensaries in assertions are those which are given as reasons for visits to these health resources (for additional descriptions of the study, see Clement 1974; see also Stefflre 1972 and P. Kay 1970). Despite these successes, the relationship between assertions and behavior has not been clear in every case. Douglas (1969), for example, found that only 5 percent of the illnesses experienced by a 3 percent sample of the Maya population of Santiago Atitlan over a six-month period were taken to a native treatment specialist even though the Maya beliefs about the "ultimate" causes of illness would seem to imply that a native treatment specialist was necessary in every case. Quinn (1974) has also reported difficulty in using elicitation methods to determine rules used by the Mfantse for setting fines in litigation. More effort needs to be devoted to the analysis of such difficulties.

[6]When the Department of Medical Services in American Samoa introduced a mental health program, it was interesting to note that the Samoans expected the program to be staffed by a special doctor who would be capable of handling severe mental disorders. At the same time they expressed a belief that severe mental problems cannot be cured. Thus, the program seemed to be a contradiction in terms. The program also had another problem. Although the program seemed to be based on conflicting premises, patients presented themselves out of curiosity in order to find out more about the program. At the time, the therapist who saw the patients held a doctorate in psychology. Because he was not licensed to dispense medication, he had to send the patients elsewhere for medication, thus violating the Samoan expectation of a special doctor. Additionally, the doctor's style of therapy, which involved extended discussions, did not fit the Samoan concept of treatment (Clement 1974).

[7]Wax and Wax (1971), for example, who have been especially outspoken critics of these assumptions, have described what they call the "vacuum ideology." The Waxes noted that educators tended to regard their Sioux students not only as lacking the prerequisite skills required by the school, but also as lacking any skills whatsoever.

[8]In relation to categorization and treatment, see also Stebbins 1970; Ianni 1974.

[9]Fortunately, cognitive techniques have been developed beyond their initial form. In the original stages of development, it was more or less assumed that

cognitive structures and beliefs were shared within a cultural population. The expectation of intracultural heterogeneity is becoming more commonplace, so that research is initially designed to handle larger samples and to test for intracultural variation. (See, for example, Pollnac 1975.) A research method incapable of handling intracultural variation would obviously not have been sufficient for the purpose of the proposed research.

[10]Even if the hypotheses examined are limited to those concerning cultural differences, there is variety. Cole and his associates (Cole et al. 1971; Gay and Cole 1967), for example, have conducted some excellent research on what they have referred to as the cultural context of learning and thinking. Another example is a particular hypothesis put forward by Durbin (1971) suggesting that black children are exposed to a type of language-learning model at home that is fully contradicted in the schools.

[11]See also Bond 1967 and M. Kay 1974 for other studies that indicate a lack of correspondence between general and specific cultural rules. In a study in which I was involved concerning urban planning in a California county (Harding, Clement, and Lammers 1972), citizens of the county revealed their ambivalence: despite their excitement about ecology as a general concept, in choosing among descriptions of alternative living environments, they rejected descriptions that alluded to the sacrifices (such as limiting car mileage) that might be necessary for a more ecologically sound lifestyle.

REFERENCES

Berlin, B., D. E. Breedlove, and R. H. Raven, 1968. Covert Categories and Folk Taxonomies. *American Anthropologist* 70:290-299.

Bond, John Raymond, 1967. *Acculturation and Value Change* (Ph.D. diss., University of Southern California; Ann Arbor: University Microfilms).

Burling, Robbins, 1969. Linguistics and Ethnographic Description. *American Anthropologist* 71:817-827.

Burnett, Jacquetta Hill, 1973. Event Description and Analysis in the Microethnography of Urban Classrooms. In *Cultural Relevance and Educational Issues*, Francis A. J. Ianni and Edward Storey, eds. (Boston: Little, Brown), pp. 287-304.

Burton. Michael L., 1972. Semantic Dimensions of Occupation Names. In *Multidimensional Scaling: Theory and Applications in the Behavioral Sciences, Vol. II: Applications*, A. K. Romney et al., eds. (New York: Seminar Press), pp. 55-73.

Clement, Dorothy C., 1974. *Samoan Concepts of Mental Illness and Treatment* (Ph.D. diss., University of California, Irvine; Ann Arbor; University Microfilms).

Cole, Michael, John Gay, J. A. Glick, and D. W. Sharp, 1971. *The Cultural Context of Learning and Thinking* (New York: Basic Books).

Conklin, H. C., 1964. Ethnogenealogical Method. In *Explorations in Cultural Anthropology*, Ward H. Goodenough, ed. (New York: McGraw-Hill), pp. 25-55.

D'Andrade, Roy G., Naomi Quinn, Sara B. Nerlove, and A. K. Romney, 1972. Categories of Disease in American English and Mexican-Spanish. In *Multidimensional Scaling: Theory and Applications in the Behavioral Sciences, Vol. II: Applications*, A. K. Romney et al., eds. (New York: Seminar Press). pp. 11-55.

Douglas, Bill Gray. 1969. *Illness and Curing in Santiago Atitlan, A Tzutujil-Maya Community in the Southwestern Highlands of Guatemala* (Ph.D. diss., Stanford University; Ann Arbor: University Microfilms).

Dorothy C. Clement 69

Durbin, Marshall, 1971. An Essay on Black American English. In *The Natural History of Education of the Black Child in the City: Final Report*, Helen P. Gouldner, ed. (Washington, D.C.: Department of Health, Education, and Welfare, Bureau of Research), pp. 65-90.

Firth, Raymond, 1959. Acculturation in Relation to Concepts of Health and Disease. In *Medicine and Anthropology*, Iago Galdston, ed. (New York: International Universities Press), pp. 129-165.

Frake, Charles O., 1964a. Notes on Queries in Ethnography. In *Transcultural Studies in Cognition*, A. Kimball Romney and Roy G. D'Andrade, eds. (*American Anthropologist* 66 (3), part 2, special publication), pp. 132-145.

————, 1964b. A Structural Description of Subanun Religious Behavior. In *Explorations in Cultural Anthropology*, Ward Goodenough, ed. (New York: McGraw-Hill), 111-131.

Fuchs, Estelle, 1969. *Teacher's Talk: Views from Inside City Schools* (New York: Anchor Books, Doubleday).

Gay, John, and Michael Cole, 1967. *The New Mathematics and an Old Culture* (New York: Holt, Rinehart and Winston).

Gearing, Frederick O., 1973. Anthropology and Education. In *Handbook of Social and Cultural Anthropology*, John J. Honigmann, ed. (Chicago: Rand McNally), pp. 1223-1249.

————, and B. Allan Tindall, 1973. Anthropological Studies of the Educational Process. In *Annual Review of Anthropology*, Bernard J. Siegel et al., eds. (Palo Alto: Annual Reviews).

————, Thomas Carroll, Wayne Hughes, Patricia Hurlich, Allen Smith, Allan Tindall, and Sigrid Topfer, n.d. A General Cultural Theory of Education. Working Paper No. 6, Program in Cultural Studies of Education (S.U.N.Y. at Buffalo, New York).

Geoghegan, William H., 1969. Decision-Making and Residence on Tagtabon Island. Working Paper 17, Language and Behavior Research Laboratory (University of California, Berkeley).

Glazer, Nathan, 1963. The Italians. In *Beyond the Melting Pot*, N. Glazer and Daniel P. Moynihan, eds. (Cambridge: MIT Press and Harvard University Press), pp. 181-216.

Goodenough, Ward H., 1956. Componential Analysis and the Study of Meaning. *Language* 32:195-216.

————, 1963. *Cooperation In Change* (New York: Russell Sage Foundation).

————, ed., 1964. *Explorations in Cultural Anthropology* (New York: McGraw-Hill).

————, 1965. Yankee Kinship Terminology: A Problem in Componential Analysis. In *Formal Semantic Analysis*, E. A. Hammel, ed. (*American Anthropologist* 67(5), part 2, special publication), pp. 259-287.

————, 1971. *Culture, Language, and Society*, Addison-Wesley Modular Publications, No. 7 (Philippines: Addison-Wesley).

Harding, Joe R., 1973. *Cognitive Role Structure and Culture Contact: Culture Change in the Ixil Region of Guatemala* (Ph.D. diss., University of California, Irvine; Ann Arbor: University Microfilms).

Harding, Joe R., and Dorothy C. Clement, 1974. Features Affecting Acceptability of Fertility Regulating Methods in Korea. (Paper presented at annual meetings of the American Anthropological Association in Mexico City.)

————, Dorothy Clement, and Kathleen Lammers, 1972. Perceptions of and Attitudes Toward Alternative Living Environments in Santa Clara County (Report). (Berkeley: Policy Research and Planning Group).

————, 1973. An Architectural Planning Study: Prospective User Perceptions (Form and Functions) of the Proposed Ramah Navajo Learning Center (Report). (Berkeley: Policy Research and Planning Group).

Harding, Joe R., K. A. Lammers, Patti Mesner, and D. Clement, 1973. Population Council Copper-T Study—Korea (Report). (Berkeley: Policy Research and Planning Group).

Harris, Marvin, 1968. *The Rise of Anthropological Theory* (New York: Thomas Y. Crowell).

Ianni, Francis A. J., 1974. Social Organization Study Program: An Interim Report. *Council on Anthropology and Education Quarterly* 5(2):1-8.

Johnson, Allen, 1974. Ethnoecology and Planting Practices in a Swidden Agricultural System. *American Ethnologist* 1:87-101.

Johnson, James A., ed., 1973. *On the Interface Between Low-Income Urban Black Children and Their Teachers During Early School Years* (San Francisco: Far West Laboratory for Educational Research and Development).

Kay, Margarita, 1974. Ethnosemantic Analysis of Mexican-American Contraceptive Beliefs (Paper presented at annual meeting of the American Anthropological Association in Mexico City.)

Kay, Paul, 1970. Some Theoretical Implications of Ethnographic Semantics. *Current Directions in Anthropology* 3 (3), part 2:19-35.

Kluckhohn, Clyde, and Dorothea Leighton, 1962. *The Navaho* (Garden City, N.Y.: Doubleday).

Leacock, Eleanor B., 1969. *Teaching and Learning in City Schools: A Comparative Study* (New York: Basic Books).

Lounsbury, Floyd G., 1964a. The Structural Analysis of Kinship Semantics. In *Proceedings of the Ninth International Congress of Linguistics*, Horace G. Lunt, ed. (The Hague: Mouton), pp. 1073-1099.

————, 1964b. The Formal Analysis of Crow- and Omaha-type Kinship Terminologies. In *Explorations in Cultural Anthropology*, Ward H. Goodenough, ed. (New York: McGraw-Hill), pp. 351-395.

Metzger, Duane, 1973. Semantic Procedures for the Study of Belief Systems. In *Drinking Patterns in Highland Chiapas*, Henning Siverts, ed. (Bergen: Universitetsforlaget), pp. 37-48.

Nickerson, Gifford S., and Donald L. Hochstrasser, 1970. Factors Affecting Non-Participation in a County-Wide Tuberculin Testing Program in Southern Appalachia. *Social Science and Medicine* 3:575-596.

Pollnac, Richard B., 1975. Intra-cultural Variability in the Structure of the Subjective Color Lexicon in Buganda. *American Ethnologist* 2 (1): 89-110.

Quinn, Naomi, 1974. A Natural System Used in Mfantse Litigation Settlement. (Paper presented at annual meeting of the American Anthropological Association in Mexico City.)

Rappaport, Roy A., 1971a. Ritual, Sanctity and Cybernetics, *American Anthropologist* 73:45-58.

————, 1971b. The Sacred in Human Evolution. *Annual Review of Ecology and Systematics* 2:23-44.

————, 1974. Maladaptation in Social Systems. (Unpublished paper.)

Rist, Ray C., 1970. Student Social Class and Teacher Expectation: The Self-Fulfilling Prophecy in Ghetto Education. *Harvard Educational Review* 40:411-451.

————, 1972. Social Distance and Social Inequality in a Ghetto Kindergarten Classroom: An Examination of the 'Cultural Gap' Hypothesis. *Urban Education* 7(3):241-260.

Romney, A. Kimball, and Roy G. D'Andrade, 1964. Cognitive Aspects of English Kin Terms. In *Transcultural Studies in Cognition*, A. K. Romney and R. G. D'Andrade, eds. (*American Anthropologist* 66 (3), part 2, special publication), pp. 146-170.

Rosenfeld, Gerry, 1971. *"Shut Those Thick Lips": A Study of Slum Failure* (New York: Holt, Rinehart and Winston).

Rosenthal, Robert, and Lenore Jacobson, 1968. *Pygmalion in the Classroom* (New York: Holt, Rinehart and Winston).

Spindler, George D., 1973. *Burgbach: Urbanization and Identity in a German Village* (New York: Holt, Rinehart and Winston).

————, 1974. Schooling in Schonhausen: A Study of Cultural Transmission and Instrumental Adaptation in an Urbanizing German Village. In *Education and Cultural Process Toward an Anthropology of Education*, G. Spindler, ed. (New York: Holt, Rinehart and Winston), p. 230-271.

Stebbins, Robert A., 1970. The Meaning of Disorderly Behavior: Teacher Definitions of a Classroom Situation. *Sociology of Education* 44:217-236.

Stefflre, Volney J., 1972. Some Applications of Multidimensional Scaling to Social Science Problems. In *Multidimensional Scaling: Theory and Applications in the Behavioral Sciences, Vol. II: Applications*, A. Kimball Romney et al., eds. (New York: Seminar Press), pp. 211-248.

————, n.d. Language and Behavior. (Unpublished paper.)

————, P. Reich, and M. McClaren, 1971. Some Eliciting and Computational Procedures for Descriptive Semantics. In *Explorations in Mathematical Anthropology*, Paul Kay, ed. (Cambridge: MIT Press), pp. 79-117.

Stekert, E. J., 1970. Focus for Conflict: Southern Mountain Medical Beliefs in Detroit. *Journal of American Folklore* 83 (328):115-147.

Szalay, L., and R. D'Andrade, 1972. Scaling Versus Content Analysis: Interpreting Word Association Data from Americans and Koreans. *Southwestern Journal of Anthropology* 28:50-68.

Tyler, Stephen A., 1969. *Cognitive Anthropology* (New York: Holt, Rinehart and Winston).

Valentine, Charles A., 1971. Deficit, Difference, and Bicultural Models of Afro-American Behavior. *Harvard Educational Review* 41:137-157.

Wallace, Anthony F. C., and John Atkins, 1960. The Meaning of Kinship Terms. *American Anthropologist* 62:58-80.

Wax, Murray L. and Rosalie H. Wax, 1971. Great Tradition, Little Tradition, and Formal Education. In *Anthropological Perspectives on Education*, Murray Wax, Stanley Diamond, and Fred Gearing, eds. (New York: Basic Books), pp. 3-18.

Williams, Gerald E., 1973. Language in Ethnography. In *Drinking Patterns in Highland Chiapas: A Teamwork Approach to the Study of Semantics through Ethnography*, Henning Siverts, ed. (Bergen: Universitetsforlaget), pp. 48-59.

Wolcott, Harry F., 1971. Handle with Care: Necessary Precautions in the Anthropology of Schools. In *Anthropological Perspectives on Education*, Murray Wax, Stanley Diamond, and Fred Gearing, eds. (New York: Basic Books), pp. 98-117.

Applied Archeology: New Approaches, New Directions, New Needs

HESTER A. DAVIS

ARCHEOLOGY, of all the subdisciplines of anthropology, has been thought of more as a pure science than a social science. The traditional and popular picture of the archeologist is of one slightly apart from the real world (Fritz 1973:76)—the essence of the professor in the ivy-covered tower, roaming the musty museum storage rooms. Until lately, archeology has generally involved research for its own sake, and it has rarely ever been applied in the social sense at all. Its relevance (Fritz 1973) to the modern world has been expressed in general philosophic terms ("We must know where we have been in order to know where we are going." "A country without a past is like a man without a memory."), a level usually unsatisfactory to the nonarcheologist.

Archeology has had, of course, its own peculiar history relevant to the outside world: it is one of the few sciences (the other always mentioned is astronomy) to which persons with no formal academic training can make outstanding contributions; it has been highly successful in a few extremely visible instances in interpreting the past to the general public (e.g., Williamsburg, Mesa Verde); it has been misrepresented, misunderstood, and maligned in all of the public media; it is most often confused in the minds of the general public with paleontology ("What kind of a fossil is this?") or geology ("Hey, look at this colored rock I found."); it generally has the ability to satisfy the pure researcher and the curious laymen all at the same time. It shares with the total field of anthropology its contributions to knowledge of human behavior, but its data are fragile, vulnerable, finite, and nonrenewable.

Until lately, archeology could not, by the wildest stretch of the imagination, be said to have contributed significantly to the solution of social and economic problems that plague the world. While one may still question whether a study of the settlement systems in the Lower Illinois River Valley will help solve problems of world overpopulation (or even those of the Lower Illinois River Valley), there have, nonetheless, been new demands placed upon archeologists from the nonacademic world in the past five years. Interestingly enough, archeologists had nothing to do with initiating or directing the factors that have so profoundly affected the discipline—and therein lies an important lesson.

The floundering and harrassment of archeologists in the last few has made us painfully aware that we no longer live in a world of   own. There are things going on in the world around us that are affecting our research. Worse yet, a new and frightening responsibility is being thrust upon us. We are now asked to judge what is significant in that portion of the past that remains to us. What we say is of significance now may actually be preserved; what we say is not significant, or what we ignore, will probably be destroyed. This responsibility will mean that decisions we make now will determine what is saved of the evidence of the past.

If we ignore this responsibility, if we keep our heads stuck in our one-meter pits, others will destroy the evidence needed to reconstruct the past. I cannot wholeheartedly agree that we must shoulder this responsibility for the sake of the discipline (Lipe 1974); our responsibility in this realm is to future generations. If we do not get involved, the raw data will be destroyed, the discipline will atrophy, and our resulting demise will be well deserved. Actually, what will happen is that we will go full cycle and end up once again roaming the musty museum storage rooms.

Perhaps the most important factor affecting the recent directions of archeology—and probably affecting them for a good while to come— was the passage in 1969 of the National Environmental Policy Act. No archeologist had anything to do with drafting this legislation; indeed, archeology is not specifically mentioned in the act at all. But all interpretations and applications of the law have assumed that archeological resources are a part of the "historic, cultural, and natural aspects of our national heritage." In complying with this law, then, federal agencies, and anyone using federal funds, must consider archeological resources when they assess the effect of their project on the environment. The law was written presumably with the public good in mind and as an expression of national policy. It has created needs on the part of nonarcheologists which have nothing to do with basic academic archeological research. The agencies' first concern is with compliance with the law so that they can get on with their job. Nonarcheologists are asking for specific information from archeologists based on wording in the law, wording which was not written by archeologists and which basically was written to apply to different kinds of data. The words "assess the significance" and "determine the value" of environmental resources are now being applied to archeological resources as well.

Agencies justifiably assume that archeologists can provide them with this information. Not being aware of the nuances of archeological research, they assume that once an archeological site has been located its significance can be assessed. Initially, archeologists thought so too, until it became clear that significance is a relative thing—what is significant to the archeologist might not seem significant to the Corps of Engineers; what is significant to one archeologist may not be significant to another; what is significant today may not be significant tomorrow. It was soon obvious that although the agencies might not feel they should get into basic scientific archeological research, archeologists could not provide them with the information they needed without such research. The outside world is having a profound effect upon archeological research.

As it happens, another piece of federal legislation, passed in 1966, is involved in the problems of agency compliance with the law and with archeological information needed for compliance. At first glance it seemed to help us with the knotty problem of defining significance. This law, the National Historic Preservation Act, specifically mentions archeology, or more correctly, archeological sites, but again, it was not conceived and written by archeologists. Its provisions that affect archeology were written more with historic and architectural sites in mind. However, in expanding the National Register of Historic Places, it does include some specific criteria for judging whether sites are of such significance that they should be included on the register. There are four criteria, and it is the last which specifically applies to the interests of archeologists:

> The quality of significance in American history, architecture, archeology, and culture is present in districts, sites, buildings, structures, and objects of State and local importance that possess integrity of location, design, setting, materials, workmanship, feeling and association, and:
> (1) That are associated with events that have made a significant contribution to the broad patterns of our history; or
> (2) That are associated with the lives of persons significant in our past; or
> (3) That embody the distinctive characteristics of a type, period, or

method of construction, or that represent the work of a master, or that possess high artistic values, or that represent a significant and distinguishable entity whose components may lack individual distinctions; or

(4) That have yielded, or may be likely to yield, information important in prehistory or history. (*Federal Register*, January 25, 1974: 3369)

If we interpret this final criterion in its broad general terms, then all archeological sites are eligible for nomination to the National Register. Who among us would be willing to say that a site *may not* "be likely to yield information important in prehistory or history," particularly if all the information one has from the site is from surface collections? To anyone who has been involved in preparing a nomination form for the register, it is mind-boggling to imagine putting all known sites on the register. What we had hoped might be helpful to us, is, in fact, when taken to its logical conclusion, supremely unrealistic.

Nevertheless, placement of a site on the National Register or determination of its eligibility for nomination is one of the very few means of affording it any kind of protection from potential destruction. Granted, this is protection only from destruction by a federal agency or an agency using federal funds or permits, and in the last analysis, the agency makes the final decision (unless the courts have something to say) as to whether a project will continue as planned. But putting a site on the National Register assures that it will be given due consideration, since by virtue of its nomination it has been declared significant.

Here, then, is a mechanism for protection of sites thrust into archeologists' hands but conceived by others. Its application to archeological information has meant some tortuous thinking and has demanded some new approaches in order to make maximum use of this protective device.

In order to protect a site through registration, we must determine its significance. Normally, an archeologist determines significance through investigation of the information contained in a site, i.e., through excavation. Excavation destroys the site in the meaning of the word that historians use—that is, a particular geographic spot in the earth. If it is destroyed, then it is no longer a site, in the National Register sense, and should be removed from the listing. On the other hand, if it is possible to determine the significance of a site to the extent of indicating that it is eligible for nomination, this means it is significant enough that it should not be destroyed by a federal project. In that event, it should not be destroyed through excavation either.

If we follow through with this protective mechanism, we are preserving sites but eliminating them from our own further investigation.

The basic question, then, affecting the directions and approaches of archeology is: What are the circumstances under which the archeologist can determine the significance of the archeological resources in a site? Attendant upon this question are others of a less academic nature: How much and what kinds of information are needed by agencies to comply with the law? Under what circumstances should threatened sites be excavated or nominated to the National Register? These are questions that must be answered not only with the archeological resources in mind but with the total public good in mind as well. They are not questions archeologists have had to deal with in the past, and to my knowledge they have yet to be satisfactorily answered.

Archeologists' relations with the federal government in the past have been informal. We have sent profound proposals to the National Science Foundation (NSF) for pure research on particular topics, and although we are obliged to tell NSF what resulted from their investment, there was little auditing of the books, no request for a lengthy, detailed, and formal report. For the last twenty-five years we have worked closely with the National Park Service to salvage materials and information that would be affected by Corps of Engineers reservoir projects. The Park Service would tell us how much money they had budgeted for work in a particular reservoir that year, and we would provide a proposal and a budget for a season of work. At the end of the fieldwork, we could bill for 90 percent of the contract funds and ask for an extension on completion of the report because things were taking longer than we had anticipated. We did have to submit a publishable report before we (or rather our institution) were paid the final 10 percent of the funds. We were lulled into innocence by these benevolent agencies, who were concerned with research per se and in preserving information, and not with compliance with a particular law. These agencies had no other primary archeological responsibility than to fund research for a specific purpose. Not so the federal agencies with whom we now must relate. They must consider environmental resources before they can get on with the job for which they were created. Their approach, their needs, their methods for dealing with us are totally different from what we have experienced in the past. There are now lengthy contract negotiations; the agency itself presents the archeologist with contract specifications; agencies are requesting bids for work; archeological institutions are being treated on the same basis as archi-tectural-engineering firms who have been doing contractual studies for federal agencies for a long time. This is requiring, quite obviously, new approaches, new needs, and new methods for archeologists. We must maintain our commitment to the scholarly discipline, and we feel a need to maintain control over our own destiny. We seem to have come through the prelude bloodied and wavering but resilient enough to pull ourselves together and respond to the changing times.

What, indeed, have archeologists been doing to respond to this new world, one in which they must apply their talents and expertise to a whole new set of problems?

Initially, the response was essentially forced upon us by the passage of the Historic Preservation Act, which opened up the way for states to get into the preservation field, including archeological preservation. States were required to prepare a State Plan for Historic Preservation, and preservation of archeological resources was to be included in this plan. It has been eye-opening and mind-opening for archeologists to plan on this level, rather than on a small functional or topical frame-work or geographical area. Archeologists actually have been extremely slow in recognizing the usefulness of this approach and the need for their input into this kind of planning.

Perhaps the most heartening response to this outside pressure has been brought forth by the archeologists' need to talk to each other—to find out how other people were responding to a request for a bid on a project or a request for a study that contained totally unrealistic archeological specifications because they had been drawn up by a structural engineer. There are really startling changes in the ways archeologists are relating to each other—to be specific, there are two new phenomena within the discipline in this regard. The first is a new kind of organizational meeting, one dealing not with the presenta-tion of scholarly papers for the purpose of exchanging technical and theoretical ideas, but one designed to share approaches and ideas in dealing with the demands and needs brought about by the new legisla-tion (Lipe and Lindsay 1974). (This is, incidently, a phenomenon of the Midwest and West, not as yet of the East!) The other change can be seen as promising a bright new era in the profession; it is the organization of state councils of archeology. For the first time, archeologists employed by or with research interests within a parti-cular state are banding together, sometimes into incorporated units, essentially for the purpose of exercising some control over the preservation or destruction of resources within that state. They are endeavoring to establish priorities for and approaches to the research being done, to spread the work load in the most efficient manner, and in general are cooperating in a way not seen in the profession before. It bodes well for a logical, efficient approach to the conservation, protection, and exploitation of our resource base.

Archeologists are responding in a more traditional manner also, that is, within the hallowed walls of the country's academic institutions. Most contract work is done through academic instituions, of course, so it is the academic archeologist who is often harrassed with the new problems I have outlined above. The scholarly archeologists are learning by doing and are recognizing that it is imperative that they prepare future archeologists to handle effectively the new approaches affecting archeological research. The need for specialists at the master's level is being recognized. As a consequence, some graduate departments are rethinking their programs.

There is no doubt in my mind that all new approaches and methods required by these new needs must rest on a firm grounding in the academic discipline of anthropology. While I strongly urge the development of programs that prepare archeologists for the situations they will have to face, I don't believe it can be done through narrow attention to archeological problems alone. It seems important for archeologists to remain anthropologists in their approach to their data, so that no matter what the instigating mechanism or the financial source for their research, their professional commitment remains intact. In fact from my own experience, I feel that my master's degree in cultural anthropology has probably better prepared me for the administrative job I now hold than would the traditional M.A. in archeology. I am probably better able to deal with people in the nonacademic world than if my whole scholarly training had been oriented toward handling pots and points. I can fully attest that an understanding of modern social and economic systems and a grounding in cultural relativism is of tremendous benefit to any archeologist now faced with relating to the Soil Conservation Service or the Bureau of Land Management.

Major sweeping changes in graduate programs will be slow to materialize, but something is already working its way into traditional programs in many parts of the country—and that is a specialized seminar in public archeology. Exactly what this involves in each instance undoubtedly depends upon the experience of the instructor, but to my knowledge at least half a dozen such courses are being taught currently. The important point is that what these courses are teaching is, indeed, applied archeology. They consider how best to apply basic knowledge of archeological theory and method in the context of contemporary demands upon archeologists, demands being made by nonarcheologists.

Finally, mention must be made of the profession-wide response to these changes. With the aid of a large grant from the National Park Service, the Society for American Archaeology held six week-long seminars between July and November 1974. Each was participated in by six to eight archeologists and others (depending upon the topic) and each was devoted to a topic that can only be referred to as a contemporary problem in the field of applied archeology. These topics were: certification of archeologists; report writing; cultural resource management; archeology and the law; archeological communication; and archeology and the American Indian. The first three seminars examined some very basic concerns that have resulted from the needs of nonarcheologists for archeological information. How indeed, is the Corps of Engineers to identify who is a professional archeologist; how are they to know whether the report they receive is an adequate report for their needs, or whether it is adequate in its reporting of the archeological data; how can archeologists, now that they have been given the responsibility, best manage the cultural resources of the country? It is not appropriate to go into detail on each of these here—the results of the seminars will be published by the end of 1975.

All the responses to these needs, taken together, combine traditional academic scholarly archeological research and a new responsibility toward the resources which form the basis of our research. We recognize that we have been given not only the opportunity, but a public charge to care for something that is public property—the cultural resources of the country. We must accomplish our goals and those of the public with the total public good in mind; in fact, the law says we must.

Two things have resulted so far from our tackling this new responsibility. We have borrowed a concept already used in other fields—that of management. This is not "administration," this is "management" in the sense it is used in forestry and wildlife management—wise use of the resources. Secondly, a new employment slot has been created for archeologists, i.e., the archeological managers. By and large these positions do not involve fieldwork in the traditional sense, and an archeologist who accepts a position with a federal or state agency should understand this. The archeologist may administer contracts for research done by others, but the positions require the archeologist to spend his or her time making management decisions concerning resources and interpreting those decisions to nonarcheologists.

"Cultural resource management" is a new phrase in the profession. It reflects the awareness on the part of archeologists of their new responsibilities; it reflects their efforts to control the destiny of these finite, nonrenewable resources; and it reflects the challenge of what turns out to be not a musty, dusty esoteric discipline, but a flexible, growing profession, applying itself in new situations.

REFERENCES

Fritz, John M., 1973. Relevance, Archeology and Subsistence Theory. In *Research and Theory in Current Archeology*, Charles L. Redman, ed. (New York: Wiley), pp. 59-82.
Lipe, William D., 1974. A Conservation Model for Archaeology. *Kiva* 39 (3-4): 213-245.
Lipe, William D., and Alexander J. Lindsay, Jr., eds., 1974. *1974 Cultural Resource Management Conference, Federal Center, Denver, Colorado.* Museum of Northern Arizona, Technical Series 14 (Flagstaff: Museum of Northern Arizona).

Applied Anthropology and Community Development Administration: A Critical Assessment

JOHN VAN WILLIGEN

As anthropologists attempt to develop alternative, nonacademic careers, it becomes important to assess critically their potential to perform in these new roles. Clearly, we are dealing with a variant of the symposium's focal question, which might be restated, "What are the limitations to the use of anthropology in various applied situations?" It is my intent to present a rather idiosyncratic answer to that question. That is, I will consider as systematically as possible the limitations of anthropology which I perceived while working in a specific applied situation. I will not be evaluating my own performance as an applied anthropologist per se but will consider the utility of anthropology in an American Indian community development program. The three major components of the paper will be a discussion of the nature of this specific applied situation, the role attributes of the anthro- pologist in this situation, and then an inventory of limitations and problems. The paper concludes with recommendations to the applied anthropology community, especially to those seriously engaged in training applied anthropologists. I will not treat the strengths of anthropologically trained persons in this particular situation, although there are many.

The Papago Community Development Program was initiated in 1967 to effect developmental changes of various kinds on the Gila Bend, San Xavier, and Sells Papago reservations of southern Arizona (van Willigen 1974). The program was funded by the federal govern- ment under the provisions of the Economic Opportunity Act. Organi- zationally it was responsible to a board of directors which was de- legated its authority by the Papago Council, who considered the program to be a component of tribal government. The program was based upon three key elements. The first, the community development approach, may be defined as follows:

> Community development is a process of social action in which the people of a community organize themselves for planning and action; define their common and individual needs and problems; . . . execute these plans with a maximum of reliance upon community resources; and supplement these resources when necessary with services and materials from governmental and non-governmental agencies outside the community. (U.S. International Cooperation Administration 1956:15)

The second key element incorporated into the program were multi-purpose, village-level workers selected by their communities. The third key aspect of the program was the traditionally constituted Papago village, whose felt needs were to be met through the action of the workers. A number of policies lent considerable substance to the program's commitment to community control (e.g., community selection of workers).

My involvement in the program started as a training consultant early in the program's history (October 1967). In mid-1968, I was hired by the board of directors to assist in program management and by the next year was named the Director of Community Development. I was involved in a programmatic attempt to bring about developmental change in a cross-cultural setting within a relativistic ideological framework based on the felt needs of Papago communities. As Whyte (1973:xv) notes, this represents a fairly rare occurrence in applied anthropology. More typically the anthropologist assumes the role of consultant or critic rather than principal change agent. However, both are recognized as legitimate applied roles.

The role of the applied anthropologist should be broadly defined. We can not succumb to the current "I'm more applied than you are" rhetoric that seems to be emerging with the increasing visibility of "applied types" in the discipline. Many types of applied anthropologists exist, differentiated by the approach used and the extent of involvement in applied ventures. The extent of the anthropologist's involvement can be determined through a set of categories all of which fit my folk concept of applied anthropologist.

The anthropologist is himself involved in direct action.

The anthropologist supports direct actionists through professional activity such as research.

The anthropologist carries out research for a client.

The anthropologist does policy-relevant research.

The anthropologist participates in applied anthropology training programs.

The anthropologist more or less accepts applied anthropology; at least he doesn't express open hostility.

The nature of involvement varies according to the approach used. It is possible to identify at least six major models or traditions for applied action.

The Applied Ethnology Model. Applied ethnology, the most academically oriented model, is best characterized by George Foster in his book *Applied Anthropology* (1969). It is basically the same as "pure" cultural anthropology except that a client selects the research problem. It is viewed as objective research activity, rather than as direct action.

The Research and Development Model. This model stems largely from the Cornell-Peru project and the rather remarkable capacities of Allan Holmberg to bridge the gap between individual values and scientifically based action (Holmberg 1958). The approach stresses a high level of interaction between administrative activities and research activities and makes the applied anthropologist a primary agent of change.

The Action Anthropology Model. Developed out of the Fox project, the model stresses techniques that increase a community's range of alternative paths for change while maintaining community identity and respect for the community's moral beliefs (Tax 1958). Of all the approaches it is most highly focused upon the culture concept.

The Community Development Model. This approach less clearly fits anthropology but nevertheless is dealt with in the anthropological literature (Goodenough 1963). Following the community development model, the professional stimulates and facilitates developmental change. Anthropologists involved in community development often act as consultants in training programs.

The Clinical Model. Only recently emerged, this model is still developing. The services of the applied anthropologist may be of use in a number of different clinical areas. He may provide cultural data to clinicians to improve the quality of therapy, develop culturally specific treatment strategies, assess the sociocultural cost of a specific treatment, analyze as a social system the institution providing clinical services, and participate in various types of primary clinical care

84   *Do Applied Anthropologists Apply Anthropology?*

teams. (See Rosenstiel and Freeland 1973 for a discussion of some of these aspects.)

The Community Advocacy (or Action Research) Model. This model, based on the work of Schensul and others (1973), is a recent adaptation to the urban political scene in the United States. It stresses time-effective research appropriate to the success of community actionists in improving the well-being of a specific community. This implies research that supplies results in time to be used most effectively in a rapidly changing political milieu. Research is often used to provide a factual base for community-controlled political strategies and for supporting data for writing proposals. Community advocacy anthropology aims to serve the needs of the community through its leaders rather than through an external service or development bureaucracy. Although less academically oriented, the approach is still basically a research activity.

I participated in the Papago setting as an anthropologist involved in direct action who used the community development model. In retrospect I can identify various attributes that became part of my overall role. These role attributes depict the range of activities I performed as a participant in the Papago tribal government. As an administrator responsible for managing the program, my activities involved budgeting, allocating resources, and writing reports. As an instructor I trained community development workers, which involved, among other things, planning training events for the workers. As a planner I participated in regular Papago tribal planning activities as well as in short-run activities in response to crises. As a communicator I drafted policy statements and proposals for the tribal government. I also made public presentations concerning the program. As an analyst I planned short-term research projects to supply supporting data for proposals or for political pressure. As an advisor I made recommendations to community development workers concerning various problems. I also assisted tribal leaders in formalizing their political position. As an advocate I had to try to convince Papago political leaders of the utility of the community development approach. I also undertook various activities to increase Papago welfare.

Training in anthropology, it should be noted, prepared me for relatively few of the role attributes. In fact, the difference between the performance my role required and my professional training is quite striking. I think other applied situations in which there is involvement in the action would reveal similar discrepancies between realities and preparation. The next section discusses various problem areas I confronted while undertaking my role in the Papago program. Although I stress the limits of anthropology in this setting, it should be recognized that the program was relatively successful in reaching its stated goals and was positively evaluated by the tribal government.

An inventory follows of the problems faced by the applied anthropologist in the context of a developmental change program.

Lack of Understanding of Development Concepts and Strategies Developed in Other Disciplines and Political Traditions. Numerous well-established traditions of development work (e.g., community social work, rural sociology, and agricultural extension) have produced concepts and evaluation procedures that could be of use to the applied anthropologist. Yet, as anthropologists, we tend to value our distinctive features and establish conceptual boundaries between ourselves and other sciences. Foster (1969:57-58) nicely describes anthropology's distinctive features: "most applied anthropologists feel that their most important contribution to action programs is an unusually broad and flexible field research methodology, based on a holistic view of society and culture and using general concepts such as cultural integration, cultural dynamics, sociocultural systems in contact, and the premises underlying cultural forms as a means to structure research and interpret results."

In addition to the barriers that exist between various scientific disciplines, there are limitations in communicaton between scientists and nonscientists working in development. However inadequate, "some of this social science theory proves to be, it nevertheless is not being used as fully as it might. The fault often lies with the social scientist who is unwilling to take the extra step of pointing out the applicability of his research findings to community development or anything else on this earth; the fault also lies with the community development practitioner who may not want to be bothered with anything abstract or highly analytical" (Sanders 1958:3-4).

In any case, applied anthropology training should include a wide range of concepts and approaches and stress eclectic borrowing. We cannot dissipate our energies in boundary maintenance activities. One must agree with Hymes (1974:45): "Today one should react to the utterance of 'that's not anthropology' as one would to an omen of intellectual death. For that is what it is." In the realm of application, efforts at boundary maintenance are often counterproductive and sometimes irresponsible. The focus of our concern is not our discipline, it has to be *reality*—reality mediated and comprehended through the cognitive structures provided by our continuing professional training. As applied anthropologists we should consider three components in reaching a decision to act: our competencies as individuals, the nature of reality, and the relevant ethical constraints.

Lack of a Standardized and Adequately Tested Method. There is really very little methodology that is specific to applied anthropology. Holmberg's (1958) research and development method is an important contribution but is little more than a plea for systematic data collection and a rationale for scientifically based intervention in the affairs of a developing community. In any case, the development of tested methodology should be a major goal of any research or training program in applied anthropology. The lack of standardized methods makes systematic comparison difficult and retards the accumulation of systematic knowledge. A modest first step should be a propositional inventory focused on programmatic attempts to achieve developmental change.

Lack of an Adequate Body of Theory. The existing theory in applied anthropology is inadequate to deal with all the essential aspects of the development problem in an applied situation. An adequate body of theory should contain a comprehensive set of logically plausible or empirically verified statements that explain results or predict outcomes relevant to action that is consciously planned and initiated for the purpose of achieving developmental change in a sociocultural entity. As Irwin Sanders points out,

> A review of the literature shows quite clearly the active formulation of a body of theory at the practitioner's level. This is found in community development handbooks, case studies, evaluative reports, and training materials. Its focus is upon "getting the job done," upon what works and what does not work. This practitioner's theory is set forth in lists of principles which frequently, upon closer examination, prove to be a mixture of policy statements, objectives, procedures, as well as empirically validated generalizations. (1958:3)

The theory that does exist should be extended to include the more abstract ideological aspects of development as well as the more concrete components of development such as investment rates, program design, and technology. An adequate body of theory would consist of four components ranging from the relatively abstract to the concrete: ideological assertions, principles, procedures, and means.

Ideological assertions are *a priori* basic assumptions underlying the total development concept. Often these assertions state fundamental cultural values (e.g., science should be used to improve the human condition) or articles of faith (e.g., human social systems are perfect-able). Ideological assertions provide rationalizations for development action and reference frames for consistency of action.

Principles are less abstract statements that implicitly predict such things as program success or community independence, or some other abstract goal of action. They state in general terms the conditions necessary for effective action to achieve the implied goal. Principles may condition action; they are not, however, models for action. An example of a principle follows: "Development agents must have thorough knowledge of the main values and principal features of the client community's culture" (Goodenough 1963). The goal implied here is successful development or program success. The Papago program was relatively well developed in terms of middle-level theory, mostly in the principles of community development.

The third major component incorporates procedures, a realm of tremendous diversity. Procedures are models for action. A statement of procedure provides sufficient information about processually linked developmental action to allow uniform instruction and replication of a course of action, including its result. The relative effectiveness of a procedure can be measured in terms of its goal-achievement efficiency. There is a tremendous range of procedures including technological procedures (e.g., for building a house or drilling a well) and various interactional procedures (e.g., for running a meeting or exerting bureaucratic pressures).

Means constitute the last and most concrete component of the development situation. Means are the media for developmental action. Means implement procedures. They are the tangible substances of development, such as materials, money, and equipment.

In response to the theoretical limitations we face, there should be a concerted effort to develop an adequate conceptual structure within an adequate body of theory.

The Problem of Slow Analysis. The process of problem formulation, data gathering, and generation of results in anthropology is remarkably slow. Applied situations cannot afford leisurely analysis. The problems stumbled across in a developing community need solutions quickly. As an applied anthropologist, I found myself forced into situations that at times required responses in minutes or days rather than months or years. Although I was convinced that a large portion of the solutions developed by the anthropologists working for the Papagos were effective, they were not often products of scientific processes. More often than not the solutions were achieved through dead reckoning. To quote Robert M. Pirsig:

Actually I've never seen a cycle-maintenance problem complex enough really to require full-scale formal scientific method. Repair problems are not that hard. When I think of formal scientific method an image sometimes comes to mind of an enormous juggernaut, a huge bulldozer—slow, tedious, lumbering, laborious, but invincible. It takes twice as long, five times as long, maybe a dozen times as long as informal mechanic's techniques, but you know in the end you're going to get it. (1974:99-100)

In training applied anthropologists it is essential to develop the following skills and orientations: the capacity to respond rapidly, pragmatically, and decisively, and a willingness to abandon analytical elegance, if required, to solve the problem in the available time.

Lack of Technical Knowledge. A continual problem faced in the Papago situation was our inability to control the required technical knowledge. The sociocultural problems, the stock-in-trade of the applied anthropologist, we felt competent to cope with in the Papago setting. In technical areas we were always unsure and came to depend on outside organizations for a great deal of assistance. This dependence in itself is not necessarily a problem, except that we lacked the ability to evaluate the quality of the technical assistance we received.

Lack of Understanding of the Realities of the Economics of Development. The community development approach includes a number of useful procedures for dealing with many of the sociocultural dimensions of the development situation. It does not, however, adequately deal with the question of investment rates in development. In the Papago setting the investment rate seemed to be so low that if every project was successful in a sociocultural sense, the total impact on Papago life would still be insignificant in terms of per capita income or physical development. In any case, persons concerned with development should give careful thought to the question of development investment rates.

The naiveté concerning the economics of development relates to a more general problem, that is, a tendency to overemphasize cultural explanations for program success or failure. I realize that we must consider our competencies as anthropologists in planning our activities, but we should be aware of the wider range of explanations relevant to a particular applied situation, be they economic or technical.

The Problem of Reference Group Identification. Applied anthropologists face a number of problems associated with reference group identification. As in all anthropological fieldwork, personal relationships in the applied situation require a high level of intensity. When the applied anthropologist becomes an advocate, the intensity of the relationship is often amplified. In my own experience, in order to do my job effectively, to survive politically, and to express some of my own values, it was necessary for me to become an advocate for the client community.

Certain costs are associated with the advocacy stance. It becomes apparent that certain solutions indicated by analytical results are not possible for ideological reasons (the Papago, for example, because of ideological constraints resisted efforts to prevent overgrazing). As an applied anthropologist becomes increasingly constrained by the advocacy role and ideological factors, his value to his fellow social scientists decreases. An increasing conceptual gulf may develop between the practicing applied anthropologist and the rest of the discipline. It manifests itself in intense identification with the client, perception of fellow anthropologists as exploiters of native populations, reluctance to communicate information concerning the client to other anthropologists, willingness to subvert science for the political goals of the client community, and alienation from the goals of science. This may be referred to as the Frank Hamilton Cushing effect. It need not be viewed as a problem but may in fact be necessary in certain settings. It does have an impact on the quality of the scientific concepts and analyses which applied anthropologists produce for each other, however. For example, an increasing amount of political propaganda is masquerading as science.

The applied anthropologists' intense preference for academic careers creates another major problem related to reference group identification. That is, we tend not to identify in the long run with client communities or the bureaucracies that relate to them. We seem to need to participate in academic social organizations. I would guess that an analysis of the value orientations of applied anthropologists (or perhaps their modal personality structure) would reveal a consistent difference between their values and the values appropriate to nonacademic administrative careers. For example, anthropologists seem to disparage instrumentality in human social relations. At the same time, many applied nonacademic action careers require persons to participate in social systems that have instrumental functions (e.g., development bureaucracies). This problem has seriously limited the long-term participation of anthropologists in nonacademic action careers. Because of this, we haven't been able as a discipline to demonstrate the utility of our science to potential employers, nor have we been able to set up the "old boy" networks in nonacademic action contexts so as to facilitate hiring.

The question before us, "Do applied anthropologists apply anthropology?" remains unanswered. I am forced to respond to it in a number of ways. Most importantly, if we define anthropology with self-conscious, boundary-maintaining strictness, we cannot afford to apply it. But our discipline mediates our actions, it doesn't determine them. Our actions should be based on our competencies as social scientists, the nature of the specific applied problem in its sociopolitical context, and the ethical framework which we define for ourselves. We should not be forced continually to reassert our identities as anthropologists through our actions.

In the light of this discussion and my experience with the Papago, I would like to offer the following recommendations for training applied anthropologists.

Identification with professional academic anthropology should be de-emphasized. This may be achieved through consistent contact with various types of practitioners and a high reliance on learning by doing. Student enrichment funds should be used to give trainees increased contact with participants in applied situations rather than for attending professional meetings. Training experiences that obscure the boundaries of the discipline will facilitate more effective client relations.

Applied anthropology courses should attempt to simulate the realities of the applied situation. Although this is difficult to achieve, one might consider various strategies including rigorous coursework deadlines with no incompletes allowed, developing skills in using secondary data, abandoning tests and termpapers in favor of evaluation modes that use tasks that more closely resemble the real world (e.g., writing proposals, designing an administrative structure suitable to a development plan), and reducing the reliance on projects tailored for classroom use only.

The student should not be subjected to the question "Is it anthropology?" The relevant question is, "Are you competent to perform the needed service?" With this in mind, the student should be encouraged to develop a range of competencies in social science research techniques with emphasis on time-effective methodologies. In addition, the student should be encouraged to develop competencies in areas outside the traditional anthropology department, such as systematic planning, program administration, development economics, health, education, communication, and business management.

The student should be made aware of his own values in contrast to the values of the potential client. It is absolutely essential that the student be made aware of the interaction between the goals of science, the goals of the client, and his own values. In selecting an applied career, we assume a fundamental value orientation which holds that through rational, research-based action human groups can better serve their members.

REFERENCES

Foster, George M., 1969. *Applied Anthropology* (Boston: Little, Brown).

Goodenough, Ward Hunt, 1963. *Cooperation in Change: An Anthropological Approach to Community Development* (New York: Russell Sage Foundation).

Holmberg, Allan, 1958. The Research and Development Approach to the Study of Change. *Human Organization* 17:12-16.

Hymes, Dell, 1974. The Use of Anthropology: Critical, Political, Personal. In *Reinventing Anthropology*, Dell Hymes, ed. (New York: Vintage), pp. 3-79.

U.S. International Cooperation Administration, Community Development Division, 1956. *Community Development Review*, No. 3.

Pirsig, Robert M., 1974. *Zen and the Art of Motorcycle Maintenance: An Inquiry into Values* (New York: Bantam).

Rosenstiel, C. Ronald, and Jeffery B. Freeland, 1973. Anthropological Perspectives on the Rehabilitation of Institutionalized Narcotic Addicts. In *Anthropology beyond the University*, Alden Redfield, ed., Southern Anthropological Society Proceedings, No. 7 (Athens: University of Georgia Press), pp. 97-105.

Sanders, Irwin T., 1958. Theories of Community Development. *Rural Sociology* 23:1-32.

Schensul, Stephen L., 1973. Training the Applied Anthropologists: A Consideration of the Skills Needed in Action Research. (Paper presented at annual meeting of the American Anthropological Association in New Orleans.)

Tax, Sol, 1958. The Fox Project. *Human Organization* 17:17-19.

van Willigen, John, 1974. *Development of Papago Indian Communities: Strategies, Results, and Problems*, Working Paper No. 9 (West Lafayette, Ind.: Interdisciplinary Committee on Modernization and Development, Purdue University).

Whyte, William F., 1973. Introduction: The Context of Kuyo Chico. In *Kuyo Chico, Applied Anthropology in an Indian Community* by Oscar Núñez del Prado (Chicago: University of Chicago Press), pp. xiii-xxv.

Broadcasting and
Applied Media Anthropology

E. B. EISELEIN

WE live in a media society and the most massive media within this society are radio and television. There are more radio receivers in this country than there are people, and the average radio listener spends nearly four hours a day with the medium. Virtually all American households contain at least one television set, more than half contain color sets, and the average viewer watches far more than six hours each day (Bower 1973:29).

The networks of kinship, co-residence, and social stratification are incapable of providing the massive social and cultural integration demanded by our society. Instead, integration is largely created by media. The consumption of radio and television provides the individual with a kind of social and cultural commonage with others in the society, an illusion of participation in social and political events, a common perception of the world, and a reinforcement of public opinion. Unlike the print media, the electronic media are almost instantaneous, and thus change is speeded up and becomes an integral part of the sociocultural ambience. Warner (1962) has called our society "emergent" while Toffler (1970) sees its inhabitants suffering from "future shock" and Shamberg (Shamberg and Raindance Corporation 1971) calls them "information junkies." On the other hand, Turney-High (1968) cautions against viewing the "supposedly enserfing systems" of the mass media as being as harmful and dangerous as often supposed.

Unlike many anthropologists, most broadcasters are actively involved in applying their knowledge and their skills, and relatively few engage in the full-time task of teaching broadcasting. Broadcasters use the skills and services of other professionals, including anthropologists. Thus, we have seen the emergence of media anthropology and an increasing awareness of how anthropologists can participate in the broadcasting system. The anthropologist's participation in the broadcasting system ranges from being interviewed on a news program, to assisting in the production of anthropologically related documentary programs, to doing broadcast research.

Media anthropology as applied to broadcasting provides an interesting arena for considering certain basic questions about the nature of applied anthropology. While applied anthropology has been mentioned in a great many textbooks, lectures, journal articles, and meeting papers, do we really know what is applied? Or how anthropology is applied? Or to whom? Or by whom? Must it always be associated with sociocultural changes? And finally, why anthropology? Why not some other social science?

I would like to make clear the bias under which this article is written. I am a *professional* applied anthropologist. This means that I am not a draftee simply working in an applied job for a couple of years to gain experience or to wait until the teaching job market loosens up a little. I am not a weekend warrior serving as an applied consultant while holding down a full-time academic appointment. I am fully employed in the field of broadcasting as an applied media anthropologist.

From my viewpoint applied anthropology is a profession distinct from academic anthropology. Much of this distinction lies in the area of job-related demands. In applied media anthropology the lowest priority items among the job-related demands include presenting meeting papers, writing articles for anthropological journals, and developing anthropological theories. High-priority demands are closely associated with the broadcasting industry and include such tasks as winning broadcasting awards, increasing audience size, developing programming ideas, and providing information for general decision-making.

This article is not intended to be a general theoretical statement on the nature of applied anthropology, or even on the nature of applied anthropology in broadcasting. Rather, it is a generalization based on my personal experience and is intended to illustrate the diverse tasks that an applied anthropologist can do.

I have selected three case studies in applied media anthropology for consideration. The particular cases have been selected for a number of reasons. First they differ from each other in terms of magnitude, participation of the applied anthropologist, target audience, and media. They illustrate some of the different kinds of things that an applied media anthropologist can do in the field of broadcasting. Although each case is unique, each is also typical of many similar types of projects. Second, I am personally familiar with them inasmuch as I was the research coordinator or project director for each of them.

I should like to point out one bias in the case studies. Each concerns a research-oriented project. This might lend the illusion that applied media anthropology is always concerned with research. This is not true. Many of the applied anthropology projects at KUAT-TV-AM/FM do not involve any formal anthropological research.

FIESTA was a series of twenty half-hour public television programs directed at the Mexican-American population of southern Arizona. The series, funded by the Ford Foundation, began with an admission by the broadcasters that they did not know how to use television effectively in the area of cross-cultural communication. They therefore incorporated applied anthropology into the series as another production tool.

The project called for the development of a series that would be culturally relevant and socially beneficial for Mexican-Americans. The research and production team, consisting of applied anthropologists and broadcasters, used a number of research instruments, including telephone surveys, field surveys, participant observation, media content analysis, and group discussions, to develop a basic format and some basic content suggestions.

During the production of the series, the research and production team provided audience feedback and evaluation in terms of the identification of viewers, viewer reaction, and communication effectiveness. The team continued to refine content suggestions, provide leads for the production of certain content segments, and suggest ways in which the production could increase its effectiveness in communicating to the target audience.

The FIESTA series used a magazine format in an outdoor patio set which incorporated music, interviews, film documentaries, and news. An evaluation of the series found that it had reached into three-fifths of the Mexican-American homes in southern Arizona. The final report on the project sums up the series as follows: "The case study of FIESTA has demonstrated that a public television program, designed for and with minority audience, can attract, retain, and effectively communicate with that audience" (Marshall et al. 1974:87).

SEARCH was a series of thirteen live, half-hour public radio programs focusing on solutions to Tucson's community problems. The series was intended to demonstrate the concept of programming as a form of communication feedback and hence to demonstrate the use of community ascertainment studies for obtaining program ideas.

In order to renew a broadcast license, commercial stations must undertake a community ascertainment study. The study involves surveys of both the community and its leaders focusing on the question: "What do you feel are the most important problems or needs of your community?" The license guidelines of the Federal Communications Commission provide that stations may employ outside personnel, agencies, or organizations to conduct the community survey, but station personnel must conduct the leadership survey. The Tucson Broadcasters Association provided a small grant to the applied anthropologists of KUAT-TV and AM (noncommercial stations) to conduct the community survey, to analyze the leader survey data, and to provide a demographic profile of the community for its member stations.

For most broadcasters the community ascertainment is simply another bureaucratic pain to be endured for the sake of the license. The SEARCH series was conceived as a way of showing the utility of community ascertainment studies, and by implication, the utility of applied research. Using the data from the Tucson Broadcasters Association ascertainment study, the applied anthropologist developed a basic format, selected the basic content areas, and produced and hosted the series. The series used a talk-show format and opened with a summary of research findings regarding a community problem. A panel of community leaders then explained what was being done to solve that problem and the listening audience was given the opportunity to ask questions via a telephone hook-up. A small grant from the Corporation for Public Broadcasting made possible an audience evaluation of the series.

The research undertaken for station KHOS centered on a very different problem. A frequent stereotype envisions the country-western radio station listener as a kind of pseudo-cowboy with manure on his boots, a bale of hay in the back of his pickup, a less-than-average education, a less-than-average income, and a less-than-average desire to consume the products and services of our society. According to the stereotype, the country-western listener is not a particularly good advertising target. This stereotype often plagues sales representatives for country-western radio stations. In an effort to combat the stereotype, KHOS, a country-western station in Tucson, used the services of the applied anthropologists of KUAT-TV and AM to bring out a booklet that would accurately describe the KHOS audience in terms of demography, marketing patterns, consuming patterns, and market potentials.

The KHOS study involved a mail survey of KHOS listeners (based on a list of contest participants and listeners who indicated that they wanted questionnaires) and a mail survey of systematically selected households. The two surveys provided statistical data for KHOS listeners and non-KHOS listeners. Selective use of the statistical analysis carried out by the applied anthropologists provided KHOS management with the basis of their sales booklet.

To illustrate the nature of applied anthropology in the broadcasting industry, I would like to examine the case studies in terms of the role of the anthropologist within each project, the foci of the projects and the reasons for their existence, and finally what was actually applied and how. This sort of analysis will make it possible to generalize upon the nature of the profession.

Anthropological Roles. The applied media anthropologist working in broadcasting can occupy a number of different roles. The first of these, and perhaps the easiest to fill, I call the "pure consultant." In this role, the anthropologist simply supplies information with perhaps some clarification to the broadcaster. The broadcaster then actually applies the information. This type of role is clearly evident in the KHOS project where the anthropologist simply provided the KHOS management with quantitative information on the station's audience.

The pure consultant role also appeared in the SEARCH project. In conducting the community ascertainment studies for the Tucson Broadcasters Association, the anthropologists became consultants for the association's member stations. As in the KHOS project, the station managers were given the research findings and they in turn determined how and if these findings would be translated into programming for the community.

In the pure consultant role, the anthropologist does very little applying. Instead, the station managers apply the information that the anthropologist supplies. The anthropologist has almost no control over the actual use of the research.

In the FIESTA project a new role was tried. I call this one the "team player." Here the anthropologist and the television producer worked closely together as a team in an effort to tightly integrate research and production. Whereas this approach was highly successful in the FIESTA project, it failed when an attempt to use it was made in developing a national Mexican-American public television series in the TELETEMAS project. Part of the reason for the failure was the inability or refusal of some station managers to allow social science researchers to occupy any role other than that of pure consultant. Not only is the concept of the team player unacceptable to some broadcasters, it also appears to be unacceptable to some social scientists, particularly those most comfortable in the academic ambience. They fear the intimate involvement with broadcasting production will cause them to lose objectivity in evaluating the project.

The third role I call the "fully applied" media anthropologist. This role emerged in the SEARCH project and involved the anthropologist in both anthropological and broadcasting roles. Here the anthropologist did community ascertainment research, then produced and hosted the thirteen-program radio series, and finally conducted the audience research to evaluate the series. Whereas this role is very rewarding and an efficient way of applying anthropology in broadcasting, I suspect it is possible only in conjunction with radio. Television is more complicated and tends to be a team operation.

The roles I have sketched out are merely points on a continuum. The continuum involves two spheres of concern or perhaps two social subsystems. One of these spheres is the concern of anthropology, the other, the concern of broadcasting. At one end of the continuum the two spheres are totally separate: anthropologists do what anthropologists are supposed to do and the broadcasters do what broadcasters are supposed to do. Interaction between the two spheres takes place only through the role of the pure consultant and both spheres are relatively uncontaminated by each other.

At the midpoint of the continuum, the two spheres begin to merge and the boundary lines between the two are no longer distinct. The anthropologist does some broadcasting and the broadcaster does some anthropology, both performing the role of the team player.

At the far end of the continuum, the two spheres totally merge. In the role of the fully applied media anthropologist it is difficult to tell what is anthropology and what is broadcasting. In this role, I feel, a new profession emerges, born from applied anthropology and from broadcasting. It is a profession requiring knowledge of two diverse fields—anthropology and broadcasting. Stated broadly, to be a professional applied anthropologist one must be able to function in two different fields: anthropology and some other field.

To Whom and Why. One common academic viewpoint of applied anthropology (cf. Foster 1969) sees the anthropologist studying a group of people for the purpose of introducing some sort of socio-cultural change. The work of Mexico's Instituto Nacional Indigenista; of the British applied anthropologists in Africa; and of the American applied anthropologists in Indian reservations, Mexican-American barrios, and black ghettos, all represent this type of applied anthropology. This approach can be seen as imperialistic, colonialistic, and ethnocentric in its emphasis on changing the colonials, the under-developed, and bringing them into the mainstream of society (cf. Lanternari 1974). The FIESTA project was an almost classic case study of colonialistic and imperialistic applied anthropology, hav-ing been conscientiously modeled after the programs of the Instituto Nacional Indigenista. It used public television as an instrument of directed sociocultural change among Mexican-Americans. The project fits very neatly into Foster's (1969) model of "target group," "innovating agency," and "interaction sphere." Although the FIESTA project was not unique in terms of its goals and structure, for the most part this nice neat model of applied anthropology in broadcasting is not common.

Much applied work in broadcasting does not involve any great scheme of directed sociocultural change. Thus the KHOS project studied the KHOS audience and the Tucson community, but not for the purpose of any immediately intended change. Instead, the anthro-pological data were applied to potential advertisers as a sales device to gain more advertising for KHOS. No colonialistic or imperialistic ideas about changing people guided the project, but rather, the need to make a profit in a capitalistic economic system.

Some anthropologists will undoubtedly look at the KHOS project from the traditional academic viewpoint concerning applied anthro-pology and conclude that the KHOS project did not involve applied anthropology. Nevertheless, the KHOS project is fairly typical of the kinds of things that professional applied anthropologists are called upon to do.

The SEARCH project provides a contrast to both FIESTA and KHOS. It had two basic foci. The first and most readily apparent focus was the highly educated, high-income elite that listens to public radio. The SEARCH radio series intended to increase awareness of ongoing and projected solutions to community problems. The primary study upon which the series was based, however, had focused not on the public radio audience, but rather on the entire community. The applied portion of the project was aimed at only a portion of the community. The second focus of the project, and the major one from the viewpoint of the project director, was the broadcasting system itself. SEARCH was intended as a case study to show the utility of community ascertainment studies in the development of programming. In other words, the clients and employers of the applied anthropologist were the object of the directed change.

These three projects show that anthropology may be applied to a variety of target groups and that intended change need not focus upon the people formally studied. The situation is complex and many sided. The whys of applied media anthropology may involve the ideals of colonialism, imperialism, and capitalism, or the more immediate concern with the most efficient way to get a job done.

What Is Applied and How. Just as Shamberg (1971) has characterized Americans as "information junkies," we can characterize American applied anthropologists working in broadcasting as "information pushers." In the three case studies, the anthropologists "pushed" information about the community or audience and then either the broadcaster or the anthropologist applied this information to decision-making. The quantitative information was used to make specific decisions such as when a program should be aired (FIESTA), if commercial time should be purchased on a certain station (KHOS), what topics should be covered by a public affairs series (SEARCH). Qualitative information, in the form of ethnographic and journalistic descriptions, gives meaning to the quantitative information and was used in a less rigorous fashion to make decisions concerning things like set design (FIESTA), musical styles (FIESTA), and guests for programs (FIESTA and SEARCH).

In order to obtain information about the community and audience which can be applied in decision-making, the anthropologist must use information about the broadcasting system. Generally gathered on an informal basis and depending upon who needs to know what, the information about the broadcasting system is then applied to the construction of the research design, questionnaires, and so on.

Research in applied media anthropology is primarily survey-oriented. There are two basic reasons for this. First, the communities are too large to be studied adequately in any other manner. Second, the broadcasters expect surveys and quantitative data. The more traditional anthropological research techniques such as participant-observation, lurking, and group discussions were used with some success in FIESTA but primarily for supplemental information.

Although information and research are applied mainly to decision-making, they can be used in other ways. Information can be published; it can become a part of the content of the medium. For example, in FIESTA the anthropologist frequently worked "where the action was" and consequently his field notes became a source for the news script for the programs. By the end of the series, the anthropologist carried a 16mm movie camera to shoot news footage while in the field. Similarly, in the SEARCH series much of the research information was published on the series. At the beginning of each program the host summarized the research findings concerning a particular problem as a way of setting the stage for the panelists to talk about solutions.

Most broadcasters are primarily concerned with the applied anthropologist's ability to provide information via research, but some utilize other applications of anthropology. One such application I call "perspective." In the FIESTA project, executive producer Wes Marshall summed up this perspective by saying: "While the psychologist and sociologist tend to stand back and observe the actions of a social or ethnic group, the anthropologist frequently becomes involved with the population and looks at it from within" (Marshall et al. 1974:13). Marshall credits this perspective with playing "a vital role in the success of FIESTA." The perspective is simply a "people orientation" and is applied to the development of overall project policy rather than to any specific decision.

Overall, applied anthropologists apply information about people, be it in the form of hard research data, a perspective, or a theory about human behavior. However, the information does not pertain solely to the target group, but rather must also take into account the organization itself. FIESTA, SEARCH, and KHOS were successful applied anthropology projects because they used information about the broadcasting system, information relating to the realities of broadcasting production, the needs of the broadcasters, the business of broadcasting, and so on.

After looking at the case studies and examining the role of anthropology and the anthropologist within these projects, that nagging little question remains: Why anthropology? Or perhaps, we should be more specific and ask why does KUAT-TV-AM/FM have an anthropologist on its staff? Why not someone from social psychology, or sociology, or political science, or speech communications, or communications research?

The anthropologist as a staff person in the station really began with the FIESTA project. The station needed a research coordinator for the project: someone who spoke Spanish, knew the Mexican-American community, and could supervise research. The station at this point really did not care what kind of social scientist it hired. When the station hired me, my undergraduate degree in Spanish and the fact that I lived in the Mexican-American border town of Nogales were probably more important than my graduate work in anthropology. (My anthropological fieldwork up to this time had been conducted among middle-class Anglos with a primary concern for political decision-making, social nudism, sexual behavior, and witchcraft. I had done no formal work among Mexican-Americans.) I originally began work at the station under the title Research Specialist and when identified as an anthropologist I usually met with comments like "What's that?" or "Gee, I've got an old pot at home, can you tell me what it is?" Gradually my employers learned about anthropology and I learned about broadcasting. Eventually my title was changed, at my request, to Anthropologist and this role has become institutionalized within the station.

Research is one of the primary reasons why the station keeps an anthropologist. Research provides one of the links between the broadcaster and the audience, between the broadcaster and the community. It involves audience profiles of the station and of programs aired by the station, audience response studies, community ascertainment studies, and demographic profiles of the community. By and large the research function is not particularly anthropological, but pertains to general social science. At times I'm doing sociology, social psychology, political science, or speech communication. I feel that a person from any of the social sciences could probably do the research that the station needs.

Why anthropology? Because an anthropologist currently holds that position. In other words, there is no particular reason why the station needs an anthropologist for its research position.

Perspective is another matter. The broadcasting industry gives high priority to new programming ideas, awards (together with prestige and public recognition), and increased audience. The anthropological perspective with its people orientation and its concern for people functioning in a total social, cultural, political, linguistic, economic, and biological ambience has contributed to these areas. The anthropological perspective, which often emerges under the guise of "minority affairs," is one of the reasons why KUAT-TV-AM/FM keeps an anthropologist. From the holistic involvement with people have emerged numerous programming ideas and some of the programs have won awards. Most of the programming ideas have not been directly associated with research but have come out of the anthropological experience.

Why anthropology? Because anthropology yields exciting, interesting, and award-winning programs.

In asking about the usefulness of applied anthropology in industry, Esteva (1973:95) points out that anthropology has demonstrated a concrete capacity to solve human problems. My experience as an applied anthropologist working in the broadcasting industry leads me to concur. Why anthropology? Because it works! But if it works, why aren't there more applied anthropologists?

Esteva (1973) envisions the development of an applied industrial anthropology. Similarly, Foster (1969:171) feels that "eventually, a fully developed subdiscipline of applied anthropology will come into being." How can this come about? What are the roadblocks to the development of applied anthropology?

I have some strong feelings about the *profession* of applied anthropology. First of all, I do not envision it as a subdiscipline of anthropology; I see it as a separate profession. I do not see the need to maintain the umbilical cord to the academic world and to the teaching of anthropology. I feel that our intellectual growth and satisfaction as professional applied anthropologists come from our work and the continued use of our skills.

I do not think that a graduate program in anthropology can adequately train applied anthropologists. An applied anthropologist is an anthropologist and something else. The training of applied anthropologists must include this something else and therefore must be interdisciplinary. I feel there may be a danger in training applied anthropologists with an overemphasis on social and cultural anthropology. One of the most valuable tools that I have to offer nonacademic employers is the anthropological perspective and this perspective is developed through an exposure to the traditional four fields of anthropology. Though I consider myself a social anthropologist, my exposure to linguistics, archeology, and physical anthropology has been extremely helpful. In other words, the applied anthropologists need training in five fields: the traditional four fields of anthropology and one nonanthropological discipline.

Many feel that the training of applied anthropologists should stop at the master's degree level; again I disagree. From my experience, I conclude that my station needs not only my skills but also the prestige and influence of the Ph.D. To train applied anthropologists only to the master's level is to handicap the evolving profession.

Those of us currently working and viewing ourselves as professionals encounter numerous roadblocks to the recognition and development of our professionalism. One of these exiles us from the rest of the profession. I rarely come into contact with other anthropologists and almost never with another applied anthropologist. Meetings of anthropological associations are inevitably geared to the academic types, even to the point of failing to recognize nonacademic affiliations. There is to my knowledge very little collective sense of professionalism among professional applied anthropologists and very little interchange of ideas.

Professionalism in anthropology means teaching and the assorted duties, such as research and publication, that go along with teaching. Professionalism in anthropology has implied the development of the discipline, the enhancement of science. Those of us who have made our professional thrusts in other directions have had little guidance or recognition from the existing associations of anthropologists. Although academic anthropologists and applied anthropologists may share a common background, they do not share the same professional orientation. Just as I do not see applied anthropology as a subdiscipline of anthropology, neither do I see that professional associations can realistically cater to the needs of both professions.

Associations such as the Tucson-based Mutual Protection Society for Non-Traditionally Employed Anthropologists, which calls itself "a society for professional anthros," may provide part of the answer. Part of the answer may also lie in scheduling special sessions at the annual meetings of regional and national associations. Whether with a new association or a special session, nonacademic job-related demands must be recognized. Participation in anthropology meetings is often not given high priority by our employers and hence meetings must be held on weekends so that we may attend them. Similarly, writing papers for meetings is another low-priority item in the eyes of many of our employers and I suggest applied anthropology sessions be more an informal interchange of ideas rather than a formal reading of papers.

Professionalism is the key to applying anthropology outside of the university. Academic anthropologists must recognize the professionalism of those of us who work as applied anthropologists. What is more important, we must recognize our own professionalism. The profession of applied anthropology can be an effective force within our society.

REFERENCES

Bower, Robert T., 1973. *Television and the Public* (New York: Holt, Rinehart and Winston).

Esteva Fabregat, Claudio, 1973. *Antropología industrial* (Barcelona: Editorial Planeta, S.A.).

Foster, George M., 1969. *Applied Anthropology* (Boston: Little, Brown).

Lanternari, Vittorio, 1974. *Antropologia e imperialismo e altri saggi* (Torino: Giulio Einaudi).

Marshall, Wes, E. B. Eiselein, John Thomas Duncan, and Raúl Gamez Bogarín, 1974. *FIESTA: Minority Television Programming* (Tucson: University of Arizona Press).

Shamberg, Michael, and Raindance Corporation, 1971. *Guerrilla Television* (New York: Holt, Rinehart and Winston).

Toffler, Alvin, 1970. *Future Shock* (New York: Bantam Books).

Turney-High, Harry Holbert, 1968. *Man and System: Foundations for the Study of Human Relations* (New York: Appleton-Century-Crofts).

Warner, W. Lloyd, 1962. *The Corporation in the Emergent American Society* (New York: Harper and Brothers).

In Praise of the Double Bind
Inherent in Anthropological Application

Hazel Hitson Weidman

This paper is written from the perspective of a social anthropologist with dual specializations: one in medical anthropology, the other in psychiatric anthropology. I consider myself one of a small cadre who plunged directly into these areas of specialization rather than wandering in tangentially through an "applied" door. Both orientations have been implicit in my entire anthropological experience, including my years of training in the multidisciplinary Department of Social Relations at Harvard University. From the beginning of my career, I have seen myself as a mainstream anthropologist concerned with some different types of theoretical issues and questions, rather than as an applied anthropologist. My special interests have required both a traditional department and a medical setting in order for me to be most productive and most satisfied in my career. Publications have been designed to contribute to both sides of two coins, anthropology/medicine and anthropology/psychiatry.

For many reasons I resist the label *applied anthropologist*, although some of my colleagues accept the term as appropriately describing their current work and stages of professional development. In my view anthropological applications are unidirectional and inherently transitory. Anyone who demonstrates success in anthropological applications becomes a different type of specialist and professional in the process. With successful anthropological application one loses the ethnocentrism of a strict anthropological worldview and adopts a more flexible trans-system perspective supportive of new dimensions of change (Weidman 1976). Does this, then, mean loss of the anthropological posture? Not in the least, and this is a matter to which I will address myself.

My position rests upon my own experience culminating in my present affiliation with the Department of Psychiatry at the University of Miami School of Medicine. The program developing in Miami aims at fully incorporating relevant aspects of anthropology into the training of health professionals, the structure of the health care system, and the delivery of health care. (See Weidman 1973, 1976; Weidman and Egeland 1973; Sussex and Weidman 1975.) The degree of success already achieved in the program required, among other things, acquaintance with social anthropology and its subfields of social change, cognitive anthropology, psychological anthropology, culture and personality, and culture and psychopathology. It also required acquaintance with medical systems and psychiatric theory. It has taken three years in other settings and seven years in this one to complete the first stage of successful anthropological application. Successive stages will allow for anthropological and psychiatric convergence at higher levels of abstraction than are implicit in the phrase "application of anthropology to psychiatry" (Weidman 1971).

Several key concepts are necessary to understand the Miami experience (Weidman 1975, 1976). The concept of *health culture* refers to all of the phenomena associated with the maintenance of well-being and the problems of sickness with which people cope in traditional ways in their own social networks (Weidman and Egeland 1973). It is a general term that includes both the cognitive and the social system aspects of folk therapies. Thus, health culture is composed of two subconcepts or analytic components. The first, cognitive structure, includes the values and beliefs which provide the blueprints for health action. This component requires us to understand theories of health maintenance and disease etiology, prevention, diagnosis, treatment, and cure. The second component refers to the organization of the health care delivery system. This component, which will be recognized as the social system aspect of health culture, requires us to understand the structure and functioning of an organized set of health-related social roles and behaviors. These parameters are taken into consideration in our research in Miami.

The term *co-culture* connotes parity or coordinate status. I first heard it used by Dr. Thomas Hilliard in referring to minority groups in the United States. Although subcultures may be an appropriate concept when considering groups in relation to a larger, dominant group within a nation, co-cultures is the more accurate term to use when cultural traditions are viewed from a transcultural perspective. This is the perspective adopted here.

The *culture broker* concept was introduced into the anthropological literature by Wolf in 1956. I introduced it into the health context in Miami during 1971. It proved so helpful as a teaching device that its implications for the delivery of health care were further explored (Weidman 1973). Its utility in this regard became clearly evident and led to the creation of a social status for culture brokers in a service program. The position includes components pertaining to research and training as well as to service. It is designed to elicit constructive change in the orthodox health care system as well as in various communities by means of reciprocal, negotiating types of processes.

The term *culture mediation* was introduced into our conceptual framework by Dr. Harriet P. Lefley, a social psychologist on our faculty. The term describes the processes of learning implicit in the culture brokerage aspects of the program—processes which must be made explicit in the training of health professionals.

In Miami we now have five social scientist culture brokers assisting in bridging types of negotiations in five ethnic groups in an inner-city area. We have a sixth person working in a similar capacity with a focus on the elderly. The director of the community component of the total mental health care program identifies himself as an "applied" or "action research" anthropologist.

The term *applied anthropology* or *applied social science* may appropriately describe the initial activities of the ethnically aligned culture brokers. Their current efforts are very much focused upon community organization and social change. They use anthropological concepts and anthropological skills to introduce and encourage new strategies for change in their respective communities. This is anthropological application in process. Nevertheless, in time, each will become skilled in negotiations as they pertain to a particular group. In time all will become ethnically specialized culture brokers. In time they will be functioning as more than applied anthropologists.

As the culture-broker collaboration with health professionals gains momentum, these anthropologists (or social scientists) will be functioning as more than ethnically specialized culture brokers. In psychiatrically oriented sets of negotiations each culture broker will be drawn into discussions regarding normal personality structure and functioning, matters pertaining to ego-defense mechanisms, discussions of therapeutic modalities, differential responses to medication, matters of symptomatology, and variations in forms of psychopathology. Their evaluations and their advice will be sought. And as they become increasingly effective in this aspect of their role, they will be moving toward a greater conceptual mastery of the ingredients of both systems involved, their own and the psychiatric one in which this component of their brokerage responsibility is carried out. They will, perforce, become psychiatric anthropologists as well as ethnically specialized culture brokers. By becoming psychiatric anthropologists they will be well on their way to becoming medical anthropologists. Inevitably, they will be drawn into new networks and different types of activities in the medical context.

To become professionals in an emergent field interstitial to the parent disciplines places the culture brokers in very favorable positions insofar as graduate training programs are concerned. They can as easily become involved in training graduate students from several of the applied social science programs as they can become involved in training health professionals from various medical, nursing, and social service contexts. The results of their research and their theoretical contributions will be applicable and important not only to the literature of the emerging field but also to the basic literature of both parent disciplines. Clearly, this will move the culture brokers far beyond the applied anthropology rubric, illustrating very well the transitory nature of the phase involving simply unidirectional anthropological applications.

This, then, is the direction in which our overall program in Miami is evolving. It is unfolding by design. Barring unforeseen circumstances, we will be moving in the near future toward multidisciplinary training of many types of health professionals and students from the social sciences.

It is my belief that there are fundamental double binds inherent in all anthropological applications. The basic assumption underlying this position is that anthropological applications are always directed toward culture change. This means not just change in conceptual and value systems, but social structural change as well. Success in achieving culture change of this order demands the preservation of the anthropological stance while one is engaged in becoming a new type of specialist. Can it be done? How can the dilemmas inherent in such change be resolved?

In my view, the basic "alienated" stance of anthropology must be maintained if we are to be truly successful in our applications. It is the perceptual distance from all human processes and cultural forms which counts. It is our understanding of human history, human forms of biological and cultural adaptation, value orientation, social structure, social system functioning, and processes of change which provides us continuity in our disciplinary posture no matter how far or into what fields we wander.

Within this broad framework, the specific concepts from particular subdisciplines assist us in comprehending any other social system or social setting. They allow us to structure our perceptions, to understand group behavior and cultural process—and to be sufficiently articulate in our comprehension to teach others.

Whenever we use our special knowledge to initiate change in any social context we are, of course, engaged in anthropological applications. Nevertheless, the broader perspective and the alienated posture provide us with our special flexibility and conceptual agility. No matter what kinds or forms of behavior we observe, we can always step back one more step—to move to another level of analysis, to place human behavior in a slightly broader perspective. Ultimately we can move beyond the comparative and cross-cultural to the transcultural, species-centered position beyond which we need not go in order to grasp the problems before us.

The process of establishing relevance reveals the nature of the basic double bind inherent in anthropological application. Relevance is established by determining points of congruence between the values, the concepts, and the goals of two systems. Such determination necessitates a thorough knowledge of both systems, the anthropological one and the counterpart system in which the application is to occur. This methodology of anthropological application engenders a simultaneous commitment to, yet distance from, both systems. Even though the explicit task for the anthropologist may be directed culture change, intimate knowledge of the constraints under which most social systems operate has its impact. Very often it generates respect for the many ingenious adaptive strategies at work despite those constraints.

The process of establishing relevance often leads to emotional attachment to the system requesting anthropological assistance in achieving change. There are hazards in this, because there is danger of defection from the alienated stance. Should this happen early in the change process, failure of the full applied anthropological effort is assured. Successful application requires both affective bonding and psychological distance. Most importantly, it requires a transsystem perspective, complex culture brokerage skills, and conceptual synthesizing ability. The latter is crucial for insuring stability and strength in the alienated position. It is essential for transmitting to others the potentialities of a different conceptual framework. The matter of establishing relevance is ultimately the means whereby the synthesis is achieved.

How does one manage to maintain sufficient bonding yet adequate distance to keep a concerned but objective eye on matters of relevance and areas of congruence? How, precisely, does one garner sufficient freedom to maintain the alienated stance? Consideration of these questions reveals a structural bind affecting anthropological application.

To take psychiatry as an example: Anthropologists have been invited into departments of psychiatry by chairmen who are more or less aware that a combined approach may be desirable. Frequently they have been assigned to divisions within the department (such as a division of behavioral science). This very assignment places them in line positions and prohibits them freedom to move at all levels within the social system. Such movement is essential if the anthropologist is to make his contributions relevant to the total system. A line position inherently restricts and inevitably reduces the anthropologist's impact throughout the department within which he works.

Psychiatric anthropologists have also been attached to the office of the chairman in staff positions. This appears, on the surface, to be a way of sanctioning the presence of a change agent in the department and providing him with freedom to move throughout the system, which is absolutely necessary if he is to understand its total structure and functioning. But in a staff position the anthropologist encounters a different type of limitation. Regardless of his freedom to learn where social science input might be most needed in terms of research or most congruent with existing service and training programs, he lacks the authority to insure its incorporation at appropriate places. In either of these departmental assignments, the anthropologist as change agent is caught in a double bind. No matter how much voice is given to a combined approach, the structural bind works very effectively to hinder and, at times, prohibit it. The weight of tradition, significance, authority, and prestige rests with the psychiatric side of such so-called joint enterprises. It is not surprising then, that when an anthropologist of stature in his own discipline realizes the extent to which a "joint" venture restricts the development of his greatest potential, he regains his sense of mastery and professional esteem by returning to a more supportive cultural tradition.

The solution to the structural bind in Miami has been for the psychiatric anthropologist to function at the level of consultant to the office of the chairman. Many adaptive strategies have been employed to maintain the alienated stance. Paradoxically, as will be explained below, the next stage of anthropological application will require greater bonding and less distance, for a while at least, to achieve synthesis of relevant aspects of anthropology and psychiatry in the training of health professionals, in structural aspects of health care, and in mental health care programs.

The paradox alluded to above reflects the evolutionary bind of anthropological application. This relates to the fact that what may be appropriate and functional in the early stages of application may be inappropriate and dysfunctional at a later time. During the middle period of the evolutionary process, the anthropologist dedicated to achieving the fullest success possible in anthropological applications must be prepared to back off from particularly attractive assignments, to withdraw his own presence from hard-won vantage points, to make these available to other change agents, and to move on to increasingly refined strategies in other areas.

In Miami, the psychiatric anthropologist as initial change agent has moved successfully through two of the three broad stages of anthropological application essential to achieving a full cultural transformation of the social system. In the first stage, sufficient freedom was maintained to develop research strategies, to help plan new programs, and to encourage their implementation. During the second stage (the middle period in the evolutionary process) sufficient affective bonding and adequate perceptual distance have been maintained to keep the change process in focus. Funds have been obtained and new positions for other social scientists have been secured. This required the rejection of certain key directorship positions that would have locked the psychiatric anthropologist into line positions at administrative levels below those essential to achieving full cultural transformation.

We have now reached a stage in the change process where it will be dysfunctional to the overall social system for this anthropologist to continue to maintain the alienated posture. Conversely, it will be advantageous to the system for the psychiatric anthropologist to shift into the integral position in the structure of the department and the overall mental health care training and services programs. We have reached the point at which combined skills and abilities (psychiatric/anthropological) at the highest administrative levels will make the difference in whether or not full transformation is achieved. To maintain the alienated posture at this point would undermine the total program in some respects as well as threaten every other advantage gained.

Although converging psychiatric and anthropological philosophies guide the evolutionary process, a full shift to the transcultural perspective integrating their values at a higher level has not yet occurred. Nevertheless, there has been sufficient change in the structure of the program for the department now to require conceptual synthesis to maintain momentum, funding, prestige, and stature as an innovating institution.

The time is propitious for the transcultural perspective to be diffused throughout the department, the mental health service, and professional training programs. This will involve cultural mediation in a multitude of administrative and subsystem service and training contexts. But the process of conceptual change and the internalization of new values will not proceed very well without sanctioning at high levels of responsibility and authority. Only with clearly assigned responsibility for conceptual brokerage among top decision-makers, one being a psychiatric anthropologist, will anthropological applications become more in-house and total-program oriented than has been possible heretofore. Serious efforts to mediate and link the conceptual realms of anthropology and psychiatry in subsystem contexts will enable us to achieve our goal. The subsystems involved would constitute aspects of an emerging social psychiatric cultural system based upon a transcultural value orientation.

Theoretically, there should be no problem in moving into this final stage of anthropological application in Miami. A psychiatric anthropologist was invited into the department in 1968 to work toward precisely these goals. The only difference in the social context is that seven years ago there was no way in which a professional so specialized could make meaningful contributions within the department. After seven years of unidirectional anthropological applications, a structure is now emerging in which this psychiatric anthropologist can function to the full extent of her capabilities by influencing the processes of consolidation which have begun. Unquestionably, the anthropological applications would not have been so pointed and successful had there not been combined training to build upon at the outset of this venture. The problem now is to create a coordinate social status for a psychiatric anthropologist in a department committed to anthropological/psychiatric synthesis but in which all top decision-makers for overall programming remain psychiatrists.

In the eyes of the chairman, structural limitations prohibit taking this next step. This means that unless organizational changes occur, there is no way of bringing stage two of anthropological application to closure. Stage three applications cannot begin with any great expectation of success without a declared transcultural value orientation and a departmental structure which supports full participation of a psychiatric anthropologist as one of several key policy-makers in all three aspects of departmental functioning—research, service, and training.

At the moment there is no way to predict what alternate strategies might emerge to move us beyond the particular impasse we have reached. Most certainly the program will be weakened by having the only experienced psychiatric anthropologist in the department continue in the now-dysfunctional capacity of consultant. It would be weakened even more by having no experienced psychiatric anthropologist on board at all. The dilemma confronting us is whether or not the structure can become more yielding or whether or not the primary change agent, the psychiatric anthropologist, will be rendered ineffective in this department precisely at the point of pay-off.

If the structure yields, the cultural transformation, with new service and training programs, may ultimately be achieved. If it does not yield to change, there will be considerable delay in achieving both the full anthropological application and the service and training goals of a synthesized program. In the long run both will be reached if we keep the number of social scientists that we have at present. Even if the psychiatric anthropologist should leave, the culture brokers will continue anthropological applications, as will the director of the community component of the mental health care system. However, full transformation of the overall cultural system will occur only as these individuals become more specialized in psychiatric and medical realms and are able to move with ease across conceptual boundaries to achieve the trans-system perspective which allows synthesis. It is the synthesized view that will support the emergence of new social psychiatric mental health service and training programs.

It will be recalled that I consider myself a mainstream anthropologist and resist the label *applied anthropologist*. Yet much of my effort over the past seven years has been devoted to unidirectional anthropological applications. Why, then, do I not consider myself an applied anthropologist?

Let us suppose for the moment that when I arrived in Miami, I had been new to the field of psychiatry and accepted a basic identity as an applied anthropologist. If this were my total commitment, I would be compelled to relinquish to other individuals *all* positions created in the interest of culture change. Some of the new recruits might be sufficiently well trained and experienced to approach the synthesized view required to support the new programs and new types of training we envision. Most would not be. The matter of labeling and identity is crucial. Even though I might have become fully qualified and specialized as a psychiatric anthropologist in the process of applying anthropology at Miami, I would, in my identity as an applied anthropologist be compelled to withdraw precisely at the point of fruition for the system and at the point when my own professional fulfillment would lie in an innovative professional contribution.

Does it make sense that my success an an applied anthropologist in one setting should lead only to moving on and seeking out a new setting in which to engage once more in the unidirectional process of directed culture change? Would I, as an individual, really need to hold so tightly to *only* the anthropological view that I would abandon my newly acquired expertise in a combined field and return to the security of the solidly anthropological fold? No, I think not.

In my view the distinction is basic. A psychiatric anthropologist is one who is capable of transmitting a combined conceptual approach, a trans-system/transcultural perspective, to new generations of students or health professionals. His own continuing educational process moves toward greater synthesis of two originally separate conceptual systems. The applied anthropologist, however, earns his livelihood through changing cultures, not by transmitting a body of knowledge and theory within a framework outside the traditions of the anthropological discipline itself. In my opinion, the *applied anthropologist* label (and identity) implies a proselytizing, ethnocentric posture which violates the basic, alienated, transcultural, species-oriented stance of our discipline.

On these grounds I feel that the use of the *applied anthropology* label in any generic sense to encompass such fields as medical anthropology or educational anthropology is inappropriate and inaccurate. Furthermore, I believe it a great error to use the term *applied anthropology* to refer to anything approximating a subfield within the discipline. To me, applied anthropology is a process. It should not be given the status of a subspecialty; nor should the label *applied anthropologist* be attached to anthropologists who happen to be able to use the knowledge and techniques of anthropology to help move cultural systems from maladaptive postures to more advantageous ones.

What, then, might be the implications of this view for graduate training programs in applied anthropology? It is apparent that the program at Miami and others like it are creating new job opportunities for anthropologists, in particular for those trained in medical and psychiatric anthropology. In Miami, for example, seven positions have been designed for and made available to anthropologists as a consequence of my direct impact upon the department of psychiatry. One is a research position held by an individual with master's level training. The others are for doctoral candidates and anthropologists at the post-doctoral level. These positions are currently tied to service but have research and training dimensions as well. Regrettably, we have been unable to recruit appropriately trained anthropologists to all of these positions. Only four of the seven slots are now held by anthropologists. A sociologist, a social psychologist, and a political scientist stand in the other three positions. Why should we have such difficulty recruiting the type of specialists we need, when we hear from colleagues that there is need to open up new positions for anthropologists? During a period in which economic constraints are exerting internal pressures upon the discipline to sell itself to outsiders on the basis of its expertise in culture change, why should there be such a mismatch in graduate training programs and recruitment needs?

In my view, academic departments would be well-advised to establish closer ties with programs such as ours where research, service, and training are interlocked in an intimate and productive way.

The Health Ecology Project, for example, is both a basic and applied research effort. It has made methodological contributions to a cross-cultural approach to the study of health cultures and to problems in the delivery of health care (Weidman and Egeland 1973). On the applied side, it has been involved in the planning and evaluation of health care programs. It has stimulated social structural changes in a health care system. Structural changes in health care systems bring new alignments with various communities and put new types of professionals into clinical areas within the medical institution. The integral role that such professionals play in a service context gives them advantages both for research (basic and applied) and training.

Two types of multidisciplinary training programs are now emerging at the University of Miami School of Medicine. One type focuses on specialty areas such as psychiatry and mental health care. The training program emerging in psychiatry, for example, could be the means of uniting the culture-and-personality theorists in academic anthropology with the psychiatric anthropologists who have primary appointments in medical schools.

The second type of multidisciplinary training program focuses on clinical medicine generally and relates particularly to the provision of ambulatory, primary health care. The planned facility in Miami includes the clinical departments of medicine, family and community medicine, pediatrics, obstetrics-gynecology, as well as psychiatry. The task is to provide multidisciplinary training for the health professionals who will function in such a facility. Inasmuch as Miami populations are multiethnic, it is essential to think in terms of culturally appropriate care in all of these clinical divisions.

The research potential, both basic and applied, in these emerging clinical and training programs should be apparent to all educators in both social science and medicine. In my opinion, the directors of graduate training programs in applied anthropology who sit in "traditional titanic departments" (Spicer and Downing 1974:4) should take a much closer look at what has been occurring in such fields as medical anthropology and psychiatric anthropology as they are practiced in medical contexts. Most certainly such departments should note the current mismatch of training and recruitment.

Graduate students trained in the medical contexts outlined above could move rather easily into other medical settings now beginning to adopt the Miami model. Such training could be attached to doctoral research in some selected aspect of medical or psychiatric anthropology. Peripheral types of training in action research and in the traditional unidirectional applied mode are also possible.

However, some restructuring of graduate training programs may be required for the greatest gain to accrue to faculty as well as to students. It will be extremely important, for example, to become unrelentingly self-conscious about two aspects of training pertaining to medical anthropology. One aspect focuses on substance and theory within this field. The second aspect pertains to making explicit the principles of change involved in the process of anthropological applications on the one hand and change within emergent cultural systems on the other. Both procedures are very much a part of medical anthropology. Both will contribute a great deal to general anthropological theory. These contributions should feed back into graduate training programs.

These arguments should justify the adandonment of applied anthropology as an area of specialization within anthropology in favor of a specialization in social and cultural change, the theory of which rests upon general anthropological theory. However, a special component of such training should focus upon principles of anthropological application as they pertain to social problems, to other disciplines, to emergent subfields, and to other cultures. Specialized training in fields such as medical anthropology, educational anthropology, and political anthropology could then be presented in a way that enhances their meaning for the field as a whole and insures continuing feedback to the discipline of anthropology.

The medical, educational, economic, legal, and political cultural systems are no different from any other cultural system. Why, then, should the results from subdisciplines such as medical anthropology, educational anthropology, political anthropology *not* relate back to general anthropological theory? In my view this process is inevitable. Indeed, anthropologists in emergent fields and applied graduate training programs may lead the way in counteracting the splintering influences in American anthropology and allow reunification and coordination within our own discipline to proceed. It will be with special delight that I, as both mainstream and medical anthropologist, observe the process while, it is hoped, contributing significantly to it.

REFERENCES

Spicer, Edward H., and Theodore E. Downing, 1974. Training for Non-Academic Employment: Major Issues. In *Training Programs for New Opportunities in Applied Anthropology*, Eleanor Leacock, Nancie L. Gonzalez, and Gilbert Kushner, eds. Special publication of the American Anthropological Association in collaboration with the Society for Applied Anthropology (Washington, D.C.: American Anthropological Association), pp. 1-12.

Sussex, James N., and Hazel H. Weidman, 1975. Toward Responsiveness in Mental Health Care. In *Psychiatry and the Social Sciences*, James N. Sussex, ed. Special Miami edition of *Psychiatric Annals* 5 (8):9-16.

Weidman, Hazel H., 1971. Trained Manpower and Medical Anthropology: Conceptual, Organizational, and Educational Priorities. *Social Science and Medicine* 5 (1):15-36.

————, 1973. Implications of the Culture Broker Concept for the Delivery of Health Care. (Paper presented at the Annual Meeting of the Southern Anthropological Society, Wrightsville Beach, N.C.)

————, 1975. Concepts as Strategies for Change. In *Psychiatry and the Social Sciences*, James N. Sussex, ed. Special Miami edition of *Psychiatric Annals* 5 (8):17-19.

————, 1976. A Transcultural Perspective on Alienation: The Constructive Potential of Alienation as a Concept and Transitory Condition. In *Contemporary Perspectives on Alienation*, Roy S. Bryce-Laporte and Claudewell Thomas, eds. (New York: Praeger).

Wiedman, Hazel H., and Janice A. Egeland, 1973. A Behavioral Science Perspective in the Comparative Approach to the Delivery of Health Care. *Social Science and Medicine* 7 (11):845-860.

Wolf, Eric R., 1956. Aspects of Group Relations in a Complex Society: Mexico. *American Anthropologist* 58:1065-1078.

Anthropology and the Policy Process

EDWARD H. SPICER

ROBERT REDFIELD (1963) once said that the application of anthropology enables us to test our values. I choose to interpret that, first, as referring to the values of the discipline of anthropology, although I know that he meant it in a more inclusive fashion, as a means of testing the values of our civilization. I want to talk about the values of our discipline, because I think that we have tended to make applications of anthropology on untested assumptions about these values. It has become increasingly apparent that various of us within the discipline assume that certain values characterize all anthropologists. This I agree with. We cannot have a discipline of anthropology except on the basis of a common set of values, which guides us in all we do as anthropologists, which guides us in our selection of what we study and how we study it.

However, there is a strong tendency to assume that, along with those values we hold as pursuers of a certain discipline, there is also necessarily an associated set of political values. This, I believe, is a serious error. It is a misconception despite the fact that the very subject matter of anthropology attracts year after year many students because they see our focus of study as an intellectually and morally liberating influence. The subject matter and some widely accepted generalizations in anthropology attract students who want to change our society for the better. We know this to be true and many of us go on assuming that a certain sort of liberal viewpoint about the relation between race and human capacities, about international organization and war, about bureaucracy and the people perhaps, and even about political liberalism and conservatism is characteristic of anthropologists and moreover a basic part of what has been called by Kroeber "the anthropological attitude." By and large perhaps (although I know of no one who has made the conclusive study to inform us) more anthropologists are liberal than are conservative in politics in the United States and most other countries of the world, suggesting there may be some kind of general tendency toward the linkage of a broad political position and the practice of the anthropological profession. However, we must get down to specifics in these matters, because I question whether most political issues in a given commuity are thought about or decided in the terms used in broad political categorization such as liberal and conservative.

Let me ask a few questions that may give the focus necessary for the development of the theme of this paper. Do all anthropologists agree on the question of the Hopi-Navajo land dispute now currently being arbitrated in a federal court? Did all anthropologists agree to either the policy of evacuation of Japanese Americans during World War II or the policy regarding their redistribution during the war? Do all anthropologists agree on the desirability of the program adopted at the Vicos hacienda in Peru under the Peru-Cornell project? Do anthropologists generally agree on the economic policies of the Ford administration? Or on the policies of any administration of the United States with reference to Israel and other Mideastern countries? I am not at all sure what the answers would be if I conducted a poll among anthropologists on these matters.

I believe that the answers would vary according to whether or not one had special detailed knowledge in the Navajo-Hopi case or according to whether or not one believed that the Hopis or the Navajos were the underdogs, or that the relocation of people long settled in an area is somehow wrong regardless of other considerations, or whether or not one thinks that a written commitment should always be lived up to regardless of changing circumstances, and so on.

Although there may be some tendency for anthropologically trained persons to form their sentiments within a limited range on the total political spectrum, the great majority of public, and probably private, policy decisions are not made on the basis of that set of sentiments. Faced with a problem in housing, or transportation, or health delivery, or urban growth somewhere in some specific community—or a problem in national policy vis-a-vis Israel or India or any other nation—an anthropologist takes his position in one or another of the citizen segments of opinion or as a technician aware of certain technical aspects of the problem. He votes or recommends accordingly. In this paper I do not want to go into the voting, or citizen, aspect of an anthropologist's behavior, but I do want to take up the technical side of that behavior.

I have had experience in both policy formulation and policy execution aspects of administration. I began with the second, in the

War Relocation Authority during World War II. I spent agonizing weeks in a position in which I was repeatedly in doubt about the wisdom and justice of the various turns that the program took. I was on the point of resignation at least twice, but I stayed on and have since been glad that I did. My role was that of program facilitator. While I agreed with the initial policy when I took the job of community analyst, the agency for which I worked proceeded to adopt new policies with which I strongly disagreed when first promulgated. It was at these points that I decided to resign and remained only after learning what the top policy-makers in the agency had taken into account in arriving at their decisions.

Let us look more closely at the situation in which I found myself. It was some two years after I had completed my Ph.D. and launched in a career as an anthropologist. I see this situation now as one which my training had poorly prepared me for. I also see the situation as one for which it was desirable that an anthropologist be hired. I further believe that this kind of job is of growing importance in our society and that training for it should be incorporated into our anthropology departments. I therefore present the situation as a case from which we can learn something of value for the direction of anthropology currently.

The job role can be labeled *cross-cultural interpreter*. The two cultures were those of Anglo middle-class administrators and the Japanese American ethnic group of West Coast United States. The government agency was the War Relocation Authority (WRA), which happened to have as one of its half-dozen top administrators an anthropologist, John Provinse, who strongly influenced many policy decisions. His influence was the major factor in the decision to hire anthropologists as community analysts. They were hired to interpret the Japanese Americans who had been evacuated from the West Coast to the administrators suddenly recruited from the Bureau of Indian Affairs, the Soil Conservation Service, other federal agencies, and private life. Provinse and his associates in the top policy group felt it important to have anthropologists who knew something about Japanese culture constantly at hand for administrators to consult. They became especially convinced of this when two of the camps, or relocation centers as they were called, "blew up," that is, carried out strikes and demonstrations in the fall of 1942. After those events the effort was made to equip every one of the ten camps with an anthropologist or sociologist as part of its permanent staff, and communication channels were set up between them and the directors of the local camps and with the administrators in the central Washington office.

Given the utmost freedom to carry on fieldwork and organize our reporting, we began immediately to present the administrators with descriptions of evacuee viewpoints, of situations in the newly occupied blocks in the camps, and so on. It turned out that the WRA was unable to find anthropologists who knew much of anything about Japanese culture or even about Japanese Americans and so the role of cross-cultural interpreter as first conceived became quickly modified. As anthropologists we were well enough trained to understand from the start that the evacuees would have their own point of view about what was happening to them and their own evaluations of what they could expect next from the government that had evacuated them from their homes. We dug in accordingly and followed the basic old ethnographic dictum of Boas to discover "what they thought" and get it in their own words.

In a basic sense their viewpoint was not actually understandable to the administrators, who were supposed to be solving their new problems for them, men and women who didn't have time in their fast-moving administrative duties to meditate on how the long-standing denial of American citizenship to Japanese immigrants had bent the lives of both the immigrants and their children. In an atmosphere of charges about loyalty and disloyalty in the midst of a war that was going badly at first for the Americans, the chances of understanding this fundamental condition at the roots of Japanese American lives and its implications for the new life in the centers were just about nil.

We found that we had to work at more superficial levels of interpretation. We had to report on the frictions centering on the selection of a chef in one of the common kitchens in terms of previous community connections and activities in California, but even there we had to be extremly careful about describing some of the activities of such organizations in order to avoid misinterpretation by administrators in terms of disloyalty to the United States. In short, ethnographic reporting was no simple process of description. It was a complex business of evaluating the cultural orientations of both groups and figuring out what Anglos might possibly understand of all that we learned about the Japanese American cultural orientations and situational biases for action under the new circumstances.

It was fascinating, difficult work, but I want to talk about the situation of the program expediter in the world of bureaucratic organization. For this I had not been prepared, nor had any of the anthropologists who were hired been so prepared.

Nothing in our training gave us any feel for the nature of bureaucratic behavior, the constraints that mold it, or even the functions that its different aspects serve. Some of us learned, of course, and study of that process in itself gives important insights into what had been lacking in our preparation. But this is not the aspect on which I wish to focus. I want rather to pay attention to the effects on me and other anthropologists of our ignorance of the policy-making process in big government agencies. I think our roles as specialized program facilitators would have been much better served had we had the kind of background that would have enabled us to understand this process and the relation of our reports to that process. As I reflect on this I have the sense of being very naive, but I suspect that such naiveté has been a result of the standard sort of anthropological training. Let me outline the situation, which can be dramatically seen in the particular kind of government agency which the WRA was.

Within six months after I took the job with the WRA, an important new policy called segregation was adopted. This called for separating persons loyal or disloyal to the United States. It was decided on by the director of the WRA and his close top policymakers, including the anthropologist mentioned above, in conjunction with the War Department and the Department of Justice. Essentially it consisted of classifying all those who answered certain questions on a questionnaire with a "No" answer as disloyal and sending them, whether they wished to go or not, to one of the ten relocation centers, which was then called the segregation center. All those who answered "Yes" to the fateful questions remained in the nine other camps, and those from what became the segregation center who said "Yes" were sent to one or another of the other nine centers.

By the time this policy was decided on, we analysts in the centers had done enough ethnography to know that the segregation program would not work. Of course, it could be carried out; the WRA had the power with the help of the Army to do it. But in the sense of accomplishing what it was supposed to do, it would not work. We had all done extensive interviewing, we had all been carrying on participant observation and knew that the "No" answers were made by young men and women (Nisei) who were angry, to put it mildly, at what had happened to them despite their being American citizens and yet who hadn't the slightest idea of supporting the Japanese government; they wanted merely to be fully functioning American citizens. Their "No's" were expressions of protest against what some of them called the un-American behavior of the United States government. There were at least a dozen categories, as we determined them, of "No" answerers whose answers were no indication of political disloyalty to the United States. Hence we knew that the segregation which was put into motion during that first year was not accomplishing its stated purpose and it was moreover continuing the basic injustice initiated against American citizens. I for one was against segregation on these grounds. I considered resignation from the WRA but was dissuaded because my contact with one top policy-maker gave me information about the factors involved in this policy decision. John Provinse knew as well as we community analysts did that the stated goal could not be reached in this way, because we had been reporting to him as head of the division in which we worked all that we had learned about the "No" answerers.

Over a period of weeks I learned something of the nature of the variety of factors which the policy-makers had considered, and considered carefully, in making their decision. My view had been limited to only one of those factors, namely, the opinion and behavior in the evacuee community. That is where my job centered. With the other community analysts I had been immersed in this community, learning about it, trying to interpret it in constructive ways to administrators. I saw the segregation program from the point of view exclusively of what it would do to the evacuee community, as a new wrench following close on the heels of the evacuation and uprooting leading to the relocation centers. It seemed to me unjust and cruel and, as I thought of it at first, serving no purpose except to further disrupt the Japanese Americans and probably make it impossible for them to solve their own internal problems and develop livable communities for the duration of the war. I was wrong with regard to the last point, but I did rapidly gain awareness of the segregation decision in the context in which it had been made by the director of the WRA. It then became acceptable to me, but only after it had caused me deep agony.

As briefly as I can put it, the segregation policy decision was one of a series which fitted into and made possible a broader policy on which the WRA had begun to center its efforts within six months after the evacuation order. This was the policy of keeping the relocation centers open so that all the Japanese Americans could resettle elsewhere in the United States, outside of the West Coast, which the Army kept closed. The pressures during the fall of 1942 to keep the centers wholly closed, to turn them into real concentration camps, were very great. They came from all sides, the House Un-American Activities Committee which had great influence in those first days of the war, from a more judicious Senate investigating committee, from the American Legion and other influential national associations, from the governors of various states, and from many other active groups. The finger of suspicion had been cast by the evacuation order itself and hundreds of thousands of people in the United States took that at face value.

The WRA policy-makers, however, were not ready to accept concentration camps as the solution. They resisted the permanent closing in of the centers and in 1943 got support from the Army, which had begun to have close contacts with the Nisei segment of the evacuee population. The Justice Department had been opposed to the evacuation of citizens from the start. The WRA consolidated the support from the Army and from Justice, and the policy of keeping the centers open was decided on. But unless it could be made clear that a screening process was in operation to prevent "subversives" from being sent out widely through the United States, the opposition would become more active and the general policy would be unacceptable to the Congress and various centers of opposition. Accordingly a mechanism for giving evacuees "leave clearance" was set up. The first step was administering questionnaires by the Army, which resulted in the category of "No" answerers. That led to the segregation program, which (as I became aware) the top policy-makers in WRA were almost as sure would not work in the literal sense as were the community analysts. They nevertheless regarded it as the lesser of the evils. To put it simply, they saw the greatest good of the greater number of evacuees being served by segregation. Perhaps seven or eight thousand would end up in the segregation center, but a hundred thousand Japanese Americans would be free to resettle and readjust their lives as normal citizens outside the government-run camps.

It was only as I became aware of the factors considered—public opinion over the whole United States, the tendencies toward action on the part of the Senate and the House of Representatives, an imminent Supreme Court decision that citizens could not be legally detained in the relocation centers, the changing views of the War Department, the position of the Justice Department—that I could find the decision acceptable. I had seen it only in the context of the evacuee community and a conception of absolute justice, and in those terms I could not live with it.

As I learned more about and eventually actually participated in policy-making, I could see further policy decisions in a context in which the effect within the evacuee community was one factor among many which had to be taken into account. As I became more and more aware of the overarching decision to keep the relocation centers from being turned into concentration camps, I learned to relate new policy developments to that major goal. The result, one may say, was learning to live with compromise. That is one way to put it. The balancing of factors would be another way to put it. I had to learn this the hard way. I believe that we anthropologists could have been better equipped for preparing reports that would really have contributed to policy development and at the same time we would have had a better basis for our personal decisions to stay with or get out of the agency.

A later experience saw me in the role of top policy-maker as project director of an Office of Economic Opportunity (OEO) program in southern Arizona. The program consisted in building a new community for Yaqui Indians and involved relocating Yaquis who wished to move from what had become an urban slum to a tract of suburban land given to the Yaquis for their group management by the United States Congress. A Yaqui board of directors actually constituted the policy-makers and I was their agent. However, in the very first stages of the program, they were not at all prepared to deal with broad policy-making, did not take the full initiative, and forced the policy role on me and my top assistants. It was not until later that the board of directors emerged as the effective policy body. I had had little in the way of real policy-making experience in the interim since the WRA job, my most extended experience with government administration. My assistant and I proceeded to make policy as we suddenly found ourselves faced with spending $100,000 effectively within the first year. The policy-making process was not, I regret to say, the systematic procedure that had been in operation very early in the WRA program. Little information was available regarding the factors that we dimly felt should be taken into consideration; no means were available for gathering such information before we had to make our first decisions. We had to move in some direction. That direction was strongly influenced by the general policy favored by the OEO, namely, the objective of "maximum feasible participation of the poor." My anthropologist colleague and I took this general principle seriously and developed a program that embodied our conception of it.

A great deal of information about the nature of the Yaqui community's internal organization was known. Moreover, much was on record regarding the interference of outside agents in the operation of that community organization. We knew enough to grasp how what we called the "patrons of the poor" disrupted Yaqui community life constantly through the formation of clienteles who, because of the conflicting loyalties encouraged, were not able to work together. We also knew enough to be aware that young people were directed away from the internal community life by school teachers, and we learned that this process operated even more strongly through missionaries who gained a few converts and through juvenile officers who regarded the community organization ("Yaqui culture" as they said in meetings) as the cause of the serious Yaqui social problems. We knew these things in a general way, but we knew nothing about the relations among the "helping" agencies that played important roles in furnishing the means for "disruptive patrons" to act on the community. In short, we knew much about the immediate community, and that is why we became involved, but we really knew nothing substantial about the effective social environment of that community.

Under these circumstances we developed a general policy guided far less by knowledge of the factors that needed to be taken into consideration than by a sentiment system which had, we felt, wide acceptance among anthropologists generally. This was the sentiment system that favors the underdog, that regards as good the participation of poor people, of administered people, in formulating policy affecting their destiny. This viewpoint, toward which we had a predilection was of course consistent with the policy favored by the OEO. But remember, there had been no assessment of the factors working for and against this maximum participation of the poor in the urban community where we operated. We began to feel the need for such an assessment of factors, but we had no time or staff to assemble and analyze the rather large amounts of information needed. Instead we formulated our policy in line with the general sentiment system and were launched on our course in the fall of 1966 within a matter of weeks after the grant was received.

Our fundamental policy called for training members of the Yaqui community not only to do the work of building new houses, but also to become "community workers." We gave the highest priority to training, primarily through direct experience, men and women of the Yaqui community for this role of community worker. As we conceived it, it required learning how the various agencies, private, state, and federal, that wished to assist Yaquis in one way or another actually worked and then how to mediate between these agencies and the Yaqui community. Mediation meant essentially adaptation of the agency programs to the needs of the Yaqui community as the Yaqui felt those needs. There were plenty of Yaquis of various ages, as it turned out, who were willing to undertake such training; moreover, a number learned quickly and began to be effective in the adaptation process. We set as a necessary qualification the ability to work in all three languages—Yaqui, Spanish, and English—in use in the community. We also tended to select, insofar as we were able, individuals who were not antagonistic to the dominant religious orientation and organization of the community. This excluded a few persons who had become interested in an evangelical denomination whose missionary had been working in the community. It also tended to exclude a few who had been most influenced by schoolteachers in the local elementary school. This aspect of the policy meant that our program met some opposition from among the residents of the Yaqui community. The program was, however, built on the fullest possible communication in all the languages involved with all the residents, and it quickly became apparent, after an initial effort on the part of persons outside the community to organize an effective opposition, that there was general support within the community.

The most serious problems developed promptly in connection with the larger, rather than within the Yaqui, community because of interests which outside patrons of various kinds wished to maintain within the Yaqui community. Missionaries, denominational welfare agencies, the school district officials, county and state agencies of several kinds, as well as individual non-Yaquis who had developed special relations now threatened by the community workers, all found various ways to oppose and obstruct the OEO program as we defined it. The most vocal were the Protestant missionaries. The most determined and effective were the private welfare agencies.

Our program for training Yaquis constituted a serious threat to their long-established modes of operation so long as the Yaqui community workers reported to the Yaqui board and the OEO administration and did not work under the direction of the private agency. The private welfare agency of greatest resources maintained also an interest in religious influence; the development of the community worker program, therefore, stimulated a vigorous opposition, which reached to the regional level of church organization. This in the end constituted the source of the most difficult problems in the development of the OEO program and created conditions which led after three years to the breakdown of that program. Although the physical frame of the new community became established, the building of new houses was carried forward, and a Yaqui board of directors gained experience and strength in the management of the physical development of the new community, what we had given highest priority to failed to be put on a lasting foundation.

Yaquis, at the end of the program in 1969, had no greater control or influence over their relations with the many "helping" agencies than they had before the program began. The individuals trained as community workers were able to get jobs utilizing this training to some extent, but not as mediating agents between the Yaqui community and the organizations of the larger community, which tended to submerge Yaqui group purposes in their own goals. The policy we rapidly formulated under the influence of the OEO guidelines and the sentiment system, which I, at least, believed had some kind of anthropological sanction, had failed. During this period of administrative responsibility I felt sure that what I was advocating was consistent with what I had learned to value as an anthropologist practicing my profession. It was a sense of professional righteousness that gave me strength in a situation that, in terms of practical effectiveness, steadily deteriorated as the segments of the larger community became better acquainted with what was going on in this OEO program.

These two experiences, among others, have led me to see the need for training in habits of thought not ordinarily included in departments of anthropology. Unless we stimulate such habits of thought in the anthropologists we train, I do not think that their fitness for jobs outside the academic world can be vouched for. We may train them specifically for understanding the kinds of problems that arise in connection with conflict of ethnic interests in urban environments, and we may develop ways of training for resolving such conflicts. We may train for the understanding of the consequences of rural economic development programs and in ways of preventing undesired consequences. In short, we may train for various specific kinds of jobs appropriate to persons with anthropological knowledge, but I do not think that we have laid the solidest foundations for participation in these activities so long as we ignore the habits of thought that I shall describe. Moreover, and this is most important, I do not think that we shall have made possible the maximum contribution that can come from anthropology to practical fields. It is not only the comfort, as it were, of persons in applied situations that I am thinking of or even of their greatest efficiency, it is above all the realization of the contribution that anthropology is equipped to make.

I think it is necessary to go beyond the training in basic anthropology and what most of us regard as necessary for good work in applied anthropology. It goes beyond the specific tracks being developed here and there for training in problems of health delivery, environmental impact analysis, and all the various practical fields of human resource management now rapidly being mapped out. I call it "habits of thought," because it does not involve particular techniques. It is the way of thinking that, simply put, asks whether a given goal of a given agency is better than another possible or conceivable one. It is, in short, the habit of thinking in terms of what values underlie the choice of this policy or that. This is fundamental questioning, far different from the question of how can we make this work, how can we improve upon what is being done in the framework of this or that purpose and goal.

I am saying that the process of policy-making must be studied by anthropologists as a fundamental element in their training. I am implying that the approach which says that anthropologists can be helpful in making things work better—in reducing conflict, in helping an agency to reach more widely and more effectively into the population it is trying to serve or to improve—is inadequate. I am saying that such an approach, may lead to anthropologists' becoming tools of whoever is in power in the agencies in which they work. But I am saying much more. I am saying that anthropology contains the materials in its approach and even in its present store of knowledge, certainly in its analytical procedures, for contributing to the making of public policy and also of private policy.

The making of policy is of course the putting into operation of the purposes of men. Knowledge of the process by which purposes are put into operation is essential if anthropologists are to participate in the process, whether directly or indirectly. I am advocating the development of such knowledge of the process, which I maintain requires habits of thought that anthropologists have not systematically developed and yet for which they have, as a result of the nature of their discipline, a special and eminent capacity. This is the gist of my argument; now to elaborate.

The position is diametrically opposed to that of Moynihan (1970), who after a misguided and premature analysis of the poverty programs held that social scientists should forget about policy and confine themselves to the measurement of the results of programs. To accept this advice would be to ignore the kind of questions that the best social scientists, after agonizing years, have learned to ask. It would be to ignore the modicum of knowledge we are painfully gaining. It would be to relegate social science to technical accessory activity. My position is closer to that of Peter H. Rossi (1970), who holds, after deeper experience in the poverty programs than Moynihan, that policy is precisely the area where social scientists should be working. He advocates efforts focused on experimentation with public policies in various fields, such as the maintained income experiment of the University of Michigan. I am proposing something more modest as part of training for all anthropologists. I am proposing training in understanding how the policy-making process works and what it produces. I am proposing this not with the idea of training every applied anthropologist to take a job as policy-maker or even policy advisor, but rather as necessary background for the most effective use of anthropology in all possible roles in which applied anthropologists are likely to be hired.

I propose that training be given in two areas: policy-program analysis and policy-program design. The main features of this training are that it be problem-focused, comparative, and cross-disciplinary, that it use cases based on real not hypothetical instances, and that it involve critical analysis of these instances with respect not only to whether they worked but also as to how the goals were selected. This last point contains the most important feature. It requires inquiring into the value basis of selection from among policy alternatives.

The kind of training which I envision can be thought of in terms of a course—if you will, a two-semester course. It involves an instructor and a small group of students who seek during the first semester to analyze some program in action in the region where their university is located. The aims of analysis are to determine precisely what policy is guiding the program and what value orientations underly the policy choice. An effort is made as far as possible to work out the process by which this policy was decided on through analysis of the social structure of the policy-makers. The group may proceed further into the process of program formulation and develop some evaluation technique for a rough determination of the effectiveness of the program with reference to the policy goals. This is a large order, I agree, which any public administrator will admit might result in a five-hundred-page preliminary report. However, I suggest limiting this first analysis to such proportions that it will be possible during the first semester to carry out some comparative study with an earlier phase of the program or with another regional program. A comparison comprising at least two analyses in the terms set forth would be essential.

The second semester can be labeled "Policy Design." Again a problem in the immediate region will be chosen, perhaps one of those already analyzed. The semester, with the same group at work, should result in a report on two or more possible policy goals, each to be designed with reference to what the group decides are factors of feasibility in the real situation; two or more policy alternatives must be developed and clearly specified, as well as the process by which these were arrived at. If there is time a program implied by one of the policy alternatives could also be formulated.

This may sound like academic baggage piled up a little higher and deeper. Of course, such a teaching program could become just another course among the core courses. I think two features, which should be insisted on as essential, would at the very least make it a different kind of academic exercise. At best these features would make it an active experience giving real preparation for non-academic jobs of many kinds. The first is that real programs and problems be selected on which people of the immediate region are or have been recently at work. It will be possible then to gather data not previously available but which it is decided are necessary for adequate understanding of the problem and its solution. Moreover, each semester could be a phase in an ongoing analysis of regional programs, the department becoming a continuing depository of data.

This brings us to the second essential feature of the approach. It will inevitably be discovered that anthropologists do not command the necessary information or even skills for gathering the information, almost as soon as the study begins. If the aims of the course are to be achieved, it will be necessary to establish working relationships with people in other disciplines, including the discipline that deals with citizens and public office-holders. Thus the course will require interdisciplinary interaction, that is, learning how to work in problem-solving with a variety of specialists and others. Practical difficulties need to be worked out, but we now need only consider principles.

Therefore let us pass on to other issues raised by this simple proposal. First, is it not presumptuous to propose that anthropologists set themselves up as analysts of the policy-making and administrative processes, particularly when public administrators have been trying for decades to prepare useful case books in their field? Isn't it presumptuous, when the political scientists have begun to map out as their specialty the domain of policy decision-making and have done some fine work along those lines? It certainly is a mistake to propose that we can do better what they have set for themselves as their specialties. But I do not propose that. I propose that we do something that they have not, so far as I am aware, succeeded in doing or plan to do. I am proposing, first, a comparative ethnography of the structure and functions of decision-making bodies in the field of public and private corporate policy. Second, I am proposing that on the basis of that kind of analytic ethnography, anthropologists-in-training participate in formulating policy alternatives and laying a base for choosing among the policies deemed feasible under stated circumstances. I am proposing that anthropologists get their hands dirty with value choices under circumstances that force them to experience the process as responsible policy-makers. I am not aware that this sort of approach is part of the training of public administrators or political scientists or others.

What I propose is not a part of training elsewhere because the comparative ethnographic approach and the degree of objectivity which it makes possible is simply not a part of those other disciplines. Anthropology is exceptional in the degree to which it encourages, in fact, requires, because of the scope of its data, the canvas of a wide range of goals or value orientations from which to view particular programs of action. This is true not only with respect to human value orientations but also with respect to social structures of power arrangements and of administration. I am proposing to put this approach to work on the range of human problems that extends beyond the segment that we call scientific problems. That is perhaps the most that can be said for the practical suggestion I have outlined.

Now to make it clear as to what I have not proposed. I have not proposed a new track toward nonacademic job training. The various tracks in the various areas of application are quite different things. I am proposing a basic kind of training, which should underlie the training in a particular track just as much as do the basic courses in social organization, in cultural processes, in symbol systems, and the like. I am proposing an addition to training in anthropology which will, I think, necessarily bring about other changes in our conception of what is basic in anthropology.

Further, I do not expect that such training will develop a set of policy values common to all anthropologists. I think rather that this sort of training will make it more and more clear to anthropologists that when it comes to policy decisions on practical questions, which are political, they will find a fairly wide spectrum among themselves and that training in anthropology will not produce individuals whose politics can be predicted. I do however think that this training will result in both a surer understanding of the policy-making process and also open opportunities to choose on a wider basis in one's personal politics.

I believe that this will lead to the application of anthropology, and not something else, by anthropologists trying to participate in the process of applying anthropology. For those who work in roles in which policy-making is not involved, the awareness of the policy process that lies in back of what they are doing will encourage intelligent inquiry and choice regarding the program with which they have become involved. For those who move into policy-making or policy-advising roles, of course, the value of the training is obvious. They will be prepared directly for their roles from the start. But more important than these immediate practical considerations is this: The application of anthropology must be based, if it is to be really an application of anthropology, on the widest foundation of choice among possible values in a particular real situation. The habit of reasoned choice among values can be initiated by a serious effort at policy design during the training period. The necessity for priorities in complex policy decisions, such as those in the WRA, will be familiar to the new recruit. The necessity for looking beyond a current political label supposedly identifying an ideal anthropologist will be part of the approach. Thus, I think the most that anthropology has to contribute will be realized. It is far more than a number of techniques; it is far more than certain traditional subject matters. It is an outlook that transcends the value orientations of a particular political party at any particular time, and beyond that, it is a standpoint that enables the policy-maker and his aides to step outside a particular cultural system at a particular time and to assist in giving it creative direction.

REFERENCES

Moynihan, Daniel P., 1970. The Role of Social Science in Social Policy. In *Planned Social Intervention*, L. A. Zurcher and C. M. Bonjean, eds. (Scranton: Chandler), pp. 39-47.
Redfield, Robert, 1963. *The Social Uses of Social Science* (Chicago: University of Chicago Press).
Rossi, Peter H., 1970. No Good Idea Goes Unpunished . . . . In *Planned Social Intervention*, L. A. Zurcher and C. M. Bonjean, eds. (Scranton: Chandler), pp. 74-84.

The Contributors

Michael V. Angrosino is assistant professor of anthropology at the University of South Florida in Tampa. His major interests are in medical anthropology and community health planning. His research includes studies of alcoholism therapy in Trinidad, West Indies, and of home care services for the aged in Florida.

John Bushnell is professor of anthropology at Brooklyn College, City University of New York. He has conducted a series of field studies among the Hupa Indians of northwest California and the Matlatzinca of central highland Mexico. His major interests have centered upon folk culture theory, contemporary United States Indians, and studies in psychological anthropology. With Donna Bushnell, a psychologist and psychotherapist, he is currently writing a number of papers on facets of Mexican personality incorporating data derived from projective tests administered in the village of San Juan Atzingo.

Dorothy C. Clement is assistant professor of anthropology at the University of North Carolina at Chapel Hill. Her major interests are in the areas of cognitive anthropology and anthropology and education. Having conducted fieldwork in Trinidad and in American Samoa, she is currently directing a field study of an urban desegregated school for the National Institute of Education.

Lucy M. Cohen is associate professor in the Department of Anthropology at Catholic University, Washington, D.C. Her major interests include medical anthropology, ethnohistory, Latin America, and the Chinese in the Americas. At present she is completing research on health and adaptive patterns of Latin Americans in Washington, D.C., as well as the ethnohistory of the Chinese in the lower southern United States. She is author of *Las Colombianas ante la Renovación Univer-*

sitaria and senior editor of *Patients in Programs at Area C Community Mental Health Center.*

Hester A. Davis is state Archeologist with the Arkansas Archeological Survey and associate professor of anthropology at the University of Arkansas in Fayetteville. Her fieldwork has been in both cultural anthropology and archeology, and her current focus of attention is on cultural resource management. She is chairperson of the Society for American Archaeology's Committee on the Public Understanding of Archaeology and a member of the executive committee of that organization.

E. B. Eiselein is media anthropologist for KUAT-TV-AM/FM, Tucson, Arizona. Some of his applied media research projects have included FIESTA (a local Mexican American television series), TELETEMAS (a regional Mexican American television project), MOSAIC (a local public affairs television series), and SEARCH (a local public affairs radio series). He won the Arizona School Bell Award and the Amphitheater School District Media Award for his radio series MEXICAN AMERICAN EDUCATION and the Western Educational Society for Telecommunications Best of WEST Award for his radio series ALCOHOLICS ANONYMOUS OF THE AIR. He is a co-author of *FIESTA: Minority Television Programming* (University of Arizona Press, 1974).

Louise M. Robbins is associate professor of anthropology at the University of North Carolina at Greensboro. She is interested in the effects of diverse environmental, nutritional, and cultural factors on the form and the functioning of human populations through time. In collecting data on prehistoric populations her research has taken her to many parts of the eastern United States with emphasis now on Kentucky and Ohio. She is author of *The Prehistoric People of the Fort Ancient Culture of the Central Ohio Valley* and of "Prehistoric People of the Mammoth Cave Area" in *Archeology of the Mammoth Cave Area*, edited by Patty Jo Watson.

Edward H. Spicer is professor of anthropology at the University of Arizona. His interests are primarily the study of processes of cultural change and persistence. He has done fieldwork in Mexico and the American Southwest, in Spain, and in Ireland. He has engaged in the application of anthropology off and on since 1942.

John van Willigen is associate professor of anthropology at the University of Kentucky, Lexington. His major interests are culture change and community development. He has done fieldwork among Papago Indians in Arizona and Japanese industrial managers in rural Wisconsin.

Hazel Hitson Weidman is professor of social anthropology at the University of Miami School of Medicine, Miami, Florida. She carries a joint appointment in the Department of Anthropology on the Coral Gables campus. Her major interests in medical and psychiatric anthropology have influenced a shift in her area of geographic specialization from Southeast Asia to the Caribbean and Southeastern United States. She has been engaged in both basic and applied research in an urban setting from within a medical context. Her publications have focused upon medical anthropology as an emerging field, upon comparative approaches to the delivery of health care, and upon conceptual and social structural issues relevant to achieving a degree of synthesis of the social and medical sciences in the realms of psychiatry and mental health care.

Robert M. Wulff is instructor of anthropology at the University of South Florida in Tampa. His major interests are in applied anthropology, urban anthropology, and comparative urbanization. His research includes studies of urban migration in Los Angeles, Papago housing programs, and community development in Watts, California. He is currently working with various social service agencies in Tampa designing client-oriented program evaluations.